Derek C. Hutchinson

Sea Canoeing

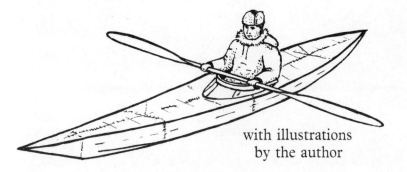

with illustrations
by the author

Adam and Charles Black · London

First published 1976 by
A. & C. Black Ltd.
35 Bedford Row, London WC1R 4JH
© 1976 Derek C. Hutchinson

ISBN 0 7136 1615 6

Printed in Great Britain by
Hollen Street Press Ltd at Slough, Berks

A man who is not afraid of the sea
will soon be drowned, he said, for he will be
going out on a day he shouldn't. But we do
be afraid of the sea, and we do only be
drowned now and again.

John Millington Synge
The Aran Islands

To Hélène

Contents

Illustrations

Acknowledgments

For a book of this nature, it is inevitable that the material will have been acquired over many years and from many sources. Much of this particular book has grown from experiences shared with sea canoeists whose skill, courage and opinions I value highly.

It would therefore be impossible to mention all those to whom I owe my gratitude. However, I feel I owe special thanks to the following:

Brian Barton, of the Corps of Canoe Lifeguards; Duncan Winning, for his generous information about Scottish canoeing; Mike Clark of *Canoeing Magazine*, for his ready help in tracing specific photographs and other research; Mr Graham, Curator of Whitby Museum; Mr Tynan, Curator of the Hancock Museum, Newcastle; the Chief Librarian, Public Library and Museum, South Shields for permission to study and draw their kayaks; Chris Hare and Chris Jowsey, for their help in some of the historical research; Phil Walton, for his mathematical brain; my daughter, Fiona, for her tireless modelling of hand positions; my wife, Hélène, for her unfailing encouragement and help in a thousand different ways—and to Mike Hanson, who said: 'Why don't you write a book?'.

Introduction

Contrary to first impressions, this book is not simply a textbook on how to progress in a particular sport. Rather it is a record of one man's discovery of a very special kind of freedom. Through the ages, man has always pursued his quest for personal freedom and has always sought to satisfy his tremendous longing to explore the unfamiliar and the unknown.

Many of the more popular rock climbs are now worn smooth by countless grasping fingers and chafing boots. Hill walks which were once a real adventure are now well-trodden scars on the grass and heather. The canoe, however, cuts no groove and leaves no scar. The same stretch of water can be paddled every day but the surface may never be twice the same. The sea provides the unfamiliar, the unworn and the unexpected. Sea canoeing gives a man the opportunity to venture on to a wild, unpredictable expanse in a craft that moves solely by the strength of his arm, directed by his experience and knowledge. Facing the challenge of the sea in this way causes a man to journey into the genuine unknown—the unknown and untried areas of his own soul. The sea canoeist depends on neither wind nor engine; he shares his craft and responsibility with no one.

The kayak man challenges the sea in what probably appears to be the most diminutive and delicate of craft, even more fragile in appearance than the smallest sailing dinghy. Nevertheless, the man who paddles the kayak well is master of one of the finest, most seaworthy crafts in the world. It can lay beam on to a breaking sea, many times its own height. The fastest and most dangerous of waters which are treacherous terrors for even the largest sailing boat or motor craft can be conquered by the shallow-draughted kayak. It can hop from bay to bay seeking shelter and finding passages where no other boat can or dare go, and it can avoid the roughest water by hugging the shore. It can capsize and be righted by the canoeist through the dextrous use of the paddle, without the man's ever having to leave the security of the kayak.

GENERAL ASPECTS

For the canoeist there are still challenges. One part of the British Isles where canoeists can find the satisfaction of discovery and the excitement of mastering wild waters is off the west coast of Scotland. Here the islands are intersected east to west, and the flood tide rushes between them, creating many dangerous passages. Here, off the northern shore of Scarba, when the tide is flooding, is the Grey Dog whirlpool. The first time I saw this, I was about 300 yd. in front of a large group of canoeists. The sea was flat calm, the sun blazing down. Between the islands I could see the surface of the water jumping and pluming in cascades of spray about 200 yd. ahead and I could hear a dull roar, like the sound of surf. It wasn't until I glanced sideways at the islands that I realised I was being swept along at a phenomenal rate. The speed with which I executed the 180° turn would have to be seen to be believed, and only by paddling with every ounce of a strength born of desperation could I make any headway at all against the fast-moving water. At last I managed to manoeuvre the boat to the nearest shore, where we all landed. A short walk brought us to a view of a terrifying whirlpool, with its surrounding violent swirls completely filling the narrow strait between the islands. What would have happened to us as a group had I not stopped when I did hardly bore thinking about.

Even more frightening is the 'Hag', the great whirlpool in the Gulf of Corryvreckan, between the islands of Scarba and Jura. The flood tide rushes through at about 8-9 knots at a depth of more than 500 ft. Where it hits an underwater rock pyramid, the top of which is about 90 ft. below the surface, the enormous surge is forced upwards to meet the mass of the upper layer of water, 90 ft. deep, forming the 'Great Race'. This rushes out into the Atlantic, turns northwards then back down the western shore of

Scarba and round into the Gulf again, only to collide with itself, forming the whirlpool of so many legends. When a westerly or south westerly gale blows against the spring flood, it creates such turbulence that the roar can be heard 10 miles away. The first waves of the 'Great Race' can be 30 ft. high and the vortex 30 ft. deep.

Paddling in areas such as this, one is dwarfed by the tremendous power of the water, yet the advanced canoeist can feel confident and secure in what must be the only small boat capable of coping with these waters.

The strength of the wind and the height of the waves and swell are sometimes such that a rescue, other than an Eskimo roll, would be impossible. You are then aware of the presence of others only when they appear on a wave crest coinciding with your own upwards rise. Communication is therefore almost non-existent: each man paddles his own lonely trip with his own thoughts, hopes and fears. He pushes himself to his limit, facing a personal test far above anything that could be devised on paper. That is why, when people say that sea canoeing is non-competitive, I feel obliged to point out that it is competitive in the broadest sense of the word. The dedicated sea canoeist aims not so much to win prizes and cups as he seeks to improve his last performance or, taking up the challenge of some difficult crossing or trip, seeks new ways to prove his own capabilities, skills, endurance and courage.

Before discussing planned canoe training, it is perhaps well to point out that it is not necessarily a difficult or even slow task to master canoeing techniques to quite advanced standards. I once found that I was short of a man for a display of canoe polo at a gala a month away. My younger son Graham was 17 years old. He was willing and I was desperate. He was given the crashest of crash courses, and by the night of the gala he could Eskimo roll every time and perform quite advanced white-water strokes so competently that no one could guess he had had only one month's experience.

It is generally accepted that there are three broad levels of competence in canoeing: the novice, the proficient canoeist and the advanced canoeist. The novice is someone who should go onto open water only when it is calm and only under the strictest super-vision. He is feeling his way in the sport, and the least change of wind or sea condition can put him in danger and place a great responsibility on the leader of his party. He is able to swim.

The proficient canoeist has been guided and instructed to handle his kayak on the sea under reasonable conditions. His boat is seaworthy for he now knows what basic equipment is needed for his canoe, his safety and his comfort. He knows the minimum number of canoeists on the sea together is three and he is able, with the assistance of his two companions of the same standard, to rescue himself should he accidentally capsize. He will be able to negotiate small waves, taking them on the beam as well as coming into shore both backwards and forwards. Any ambitious trips should be under the supervision of a competent leader.

The advanced canoeist has a high degree of skill in surf; he can plan and lead long open-water expeditions under adverse conditions of wind and tide. He can successfully Eskimo roll on the first try by a number of methods in rough water. In keeping with his knowledge and love of the sea, he has a knowledge of weather and coastal navigation, and his stamina will enable him to paddle many miles without effort. The minimum number of canoeists of this standard on the sea together is two.

It might be relevant at this point to discuss just what a sea canoe is. A canoe has been defined as 'a boat pointed at both ends, which is suitable for being propelled by one or more forward facing paddlers, using paddles without any rowlock or other fulcrum, and is light enough to be carried overland by its crew'.* In North America, 'canoe' is the name given to the traditional Canadian canoe, usually paddled with a single-bladed paddle, where 'kayak' is used only when referring to the decked-in type of craft originally used by the Eskimo and paddled with a double-bladed paddle. I usually mean a Canadian canoe only when I use that exact phrase. To me, a canoe is a slalom, a sprint or white-water canoe. The word 'kayak' in my vocabulary is reserved to mean any sea boat which has obvious origins in the skin boats of the Arctic. Having said this, if the reader finds a seemingly indiscriminate use of the words 'kayak' and 'canoe', I would plead the necessity of making the text less repetitious as well as the fact that many sea canoeists paddle slalom canoes fitted with skegs. This book deals only with

*Charles Sutherland, *Modern Canoeing*, Faber and Faber, 1964.

the single canoe or kayak, a craft in which sleep is almost impossible, unlike the double canoe, in which one of the occupants can rest, sleep or even cook food while the other paddles on.

If you would like specific advice on any aspect of sea canoeing, please write to me through the publishers, and enclose a stamped addressed envelope for a reply. Sometimes replies require drawings, so a minimum size of envelope 9 in. by 4 in. is best. The address is Derek C. Hutchinson, c/o A. & C. Black Ltd., 35 Bedford Row, London WC1R 4JH.

1
Equipment

All equipment must be seaworthy in that it must be either water-tight or able to withstand the action of saltwater, wind and rain. The canoe should be long enough to bridge the smaller wave troughs and should have a straight keel to enable the craft to maintain a course in a head, beam, following or quartering sea. Rocker (Figure 1) or the curve of the keel upwards fore and aft, enables the canoe to manoeuvre. In sea kayaks rocker must be limited, or else the boat becomes difficult to manage in a quartering sea.

Since relaxation is important when the time spent in the cockpit may be prolonged for many hours, stability is absolutely vital. This is mainly governed by the width and hull shape. Generally speaking, wide boats are stable; narrow ones are unstable.

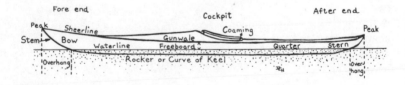

Figure 1. Parts of a canoe.

16

Hull

The V shaped or chine hull (Figure 2), the traditional shape of many Eskimo kayaks, gives directional stability so long as the amount of rocker is not excessive. However, with such a hull it is unfortunately almost impossible to maintain fast forward speeds because as the speed increases the boat tends to plane on the flat chines. The canoe thus retards itself on its own bow wave. *But as long as the bottom V is not too acute* these boats can be extremely stable and comfortable. In rough steep seas their movements are predictable, increasing confidence and allowing more relaxation than some other boats.

Figure 2. Hull shapes in cross section.

The round hull is the traditional shape of the Aleutian Islands kayaks. It is a faster shape than the chine hull because it offers less harsh resistance to the water and it gives a softer ride in beam seas. The true round hull is basically very unstable and requires skill in handling. Modern sea canoes have a modified round hull which gives speed without the unsteadiness.

Many boats have been bought with flat bottoms and wide beams under the mistaken idea that this type of stability is also seaworthy. In a flat sea the canoe does sit flat on the water but because the hull shape also follows the wave slope (Figure 3A) it is unsuitable for anything but a flat, calm sea. The round and V shaped hulls, on the other hand, can compensate for the wave slope, the shaped bottom enabling the occupant to lean into the wave (Figure 3B) for the necessary bracing stroke.

A sea canoe needs a high bow, the hull approach to which should be an acute V to slice through oncoming waves. Some full-ness in width, however, should be retained near the bow if

B

Flat bottomed boat thrown over by wave.

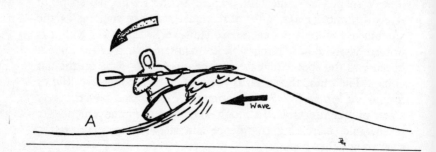

Rounded hull able to be leant into wave.

Figure 3. Behaviour of different hull shapes on waves.

possible. Extremely fine and narrow bows, although elegant in appearance, cause the kayak to plunge into the waves and thus submerge the fore end and throw spray over the paddler.

The amount of freeboard (Figure 1) should be small so as to provide little to be caught by beam winds, although the after end may have to be raised to compensate for the high bow.

Rocker

The shape of the rocker must be carefully taken into consideration in relation to the seating position; otherwise a beam wind can use the deepest part of the rockered hull as a pivot on which to spin the boat. Probably the best example of a change in the pivot point

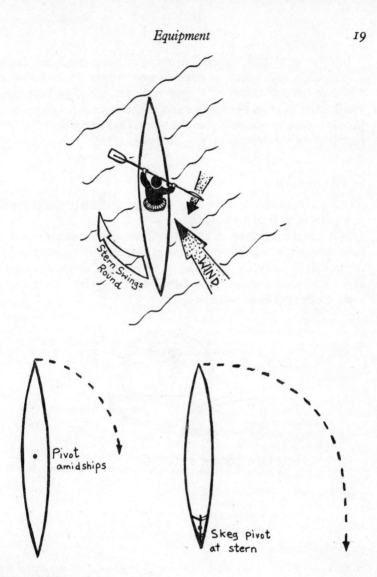

Figure 4. Pivot points.

is a slalom canoe fitted with a skeg at the rear. The skeg immediately moves the pivot point from amidships to the stern, making the boat almost impossible to turn in strong beam winds (Figure 4).

In a sea kayak this tendency to swing round is much less easily recognisable and becomes obvious only when the canoeist is paddling long distances in a quartering sea aft. The boat constantly tries to broach—turn parallel to the waves—forcing you to paddle harder on one side than the other. Over short distances the fault may be so slight as to be hardly noticeable.

Cockpit Coaming

The coaming is the lip extending out from the rim of the cockpit. It should be at least 1 in. wide.

It is not the tightness of the spray cover elastic which makes a good watertight seal but the shape of the cockpit coaming itself. A lip with a well-defined radius is better than one with only a slight curve, and pulling the fabric tightly against the smooth surface can stop most water seepage.

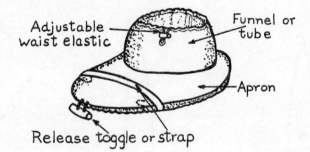

Figure 5. Spray cover.

Spray Cover

A spray cover or spray deck (Figure 5) is absolutely essential for canoeing. The paddler sits in the only open hole in the canoe, almost filling it, and by wearing a shaped skirt with an elastic around the hem, he effectively seals the hole when the cover is pulled over the cockpit coaming. Skirts made of thin wet-suit material are probably the most watertight. I use one with a very long funnel which helps to keep me warm and which can be rolled down in warm weather. But for calm summer paddling I prefer one made of neoprene-covered nylon with an adjustable elastic waist fitting. I find it does not cause condensation round my waist and if it gets really warm I can slacken the waistband.

A spray cover must have a release strap, loop or toggle so that its removal can be quick and trouble-free.

Footrest

It is essential to push the feet onto some form of footrest during the normal forward paddle stroke. For sea touring the swing-out fail-safe type is ideal because it facilitates the stowing of camping gear under the foredeck. Any strong piece of wood or aluminium tubing will do. Extra-strong footrests are hardly necessary as it is extremely unlikely that you will be standing the canoe on its end in the loop position during normal sea touring.

Buoyancy

If you bail out of an empty canoe, keep it upside down. The air trapped inside the hull will support you. However, in rough seas or surf the canoe will be rolled over, take in water and sink unless you have filled it with flotation material, in which case it will stay afloat, helping to keep you alive if you hang on to the ends, and saving you money by not sinking out of sight.

Buoyancy can be supplied by any of the following:

1. Long polystyrene blocks of foam glassed into position fore and aft are useful and they also help to support the deck. However, these can make repairs difficult and take up space which may be needed for equipment.
2. Inflatable air bags can be tailored to the shape of the canoe. These need long inflation tubes. Some of these bags have polystyrene blocks inside them as an added precaution. However I consider the plain bag best because it can be pushed in after a load of camping gear and then blown up to hold the equipment firmly inside the canoe. The blocks make this difficult. Dinghy buoyancy bags are very strong but because these have not got the long inflation tube, the one under the front deck can be difficult to place.

3. Expanded foam poured in is buoyant and useful for placing in the ends of the canoe but after a while it tends to absorb water. It never seems to dry out completely and adds more and more weight to the canoe.

4. Any flotation materials such as inner tubes, polythene wine casks, bags of ping-pong balls or beach balls will do so long as they are secured inside the canoe.

Deck lines (painters)

These lines have various uses. They can be used for assisting during rescues, for hauling and pulling the wet slippery glassfibre canoe, for holding on to in the water or for mooring. These should not be allowed to sag or come slack. Another type of line is the sort meant to be undone quickly, perhaps to pull your loaded canoe into shallow water or among rocks.

On no account must lines be fitted around or under the lip of the cockpit coaming. These can become slack and effectively tangle with the paddle in an Eskimo roll or with the paddler in the event of a capsize and subsequent exit.

Learn to splice: it makes a neat job of lines, loops and toggles.

A tow line is very handy for everyone and doubly necessary for those in charge of groups. In theory the most efficient point to tow from is behind the cockpit, but unfortunately this is a most impractical position. Towing often has to be done when conditions are bad. To swing round at right angles to the canoe being towed and then perform an Eskimo roll could cause the line to wrap round the paddle or the canoeist with tragic results. Furthermore the rear deck may well be piled high with equipment which could be knocked into the water by the sweeping tow.

The best towing point is at the stern. I include a double loop of heavy shock cord in the line, the free end of which is secured in some kind of cleat (Figure 6).

The following might make towing necessary:

1. Exhaustion when weather conditions become adverse.

2. Severe chest and arm cramps or illness.

3. Instability caused by extreme fear. One man must hold the patient round the waist to steady the canoe. The leader must then tow the two canoes to safety.

4. Need to hold speed boats and other craft from being blown onto rocks in high winds, or small rubber dinghies from being blown out to sea.

Figure 6 shows methods I have found satisfactory for the line and shock cord arrangement. But so long as lines do not foul the cockpit, and equipment secured in the shock cord is accessible from the cockpit, then experience will lead the canoeist to arrange the deck in a way which suits him personally, bearing in mind that the lines must carry out their proper function.

A. These are the grab lines. They can be on the foredeck, after-deck or both. The close-up detail of A shows how these lines can be tensioned by pulling the line tight through the loop and then knotting the line to itself, a system of line tensioning that can also be used for securing a canoe to a car roof rack.

B. The shock cord, which is just strong elastic covered with a plastic mesh, can be fed through a fitting which is fastened to the deck by pop rivets, and then be knotted as illustrated; or it can be led through a neat hole in the deck, knotted on the inside, then fibreglassed in position. There can be several cords across the foredeck, but even the farthest should be accessible from the cockpit.

C. This is a strong plastic ring and provides a smooth runner between the line A and the loop D.

D. This loop can be led through a hole in the deck and then fibreglassed in position. If the loop is used without the ring, a piece of plastic petrol tube can be pushed over the loop before it is secured, providing a smooth sleeve and preventing the line from wearing through the loop.

E. The tow line is secured to a wrap-around cleat just behind and to one side of the cockpit. A jamb cleat could also be used; these come in a number of different types and enable the line to be freed much faster than is possible with a wrap-around cleat. There should be enough line so that if the paddler needs to link up with another canoe, he can make the linking knot in front of and to one side of himself; this will invite less risk of a capsize than being obliged to tie a knot behind his back.

F. This shock cord accommodates the blades of the spare paddle, while the one nearer the stern holds the loom end. A rubber

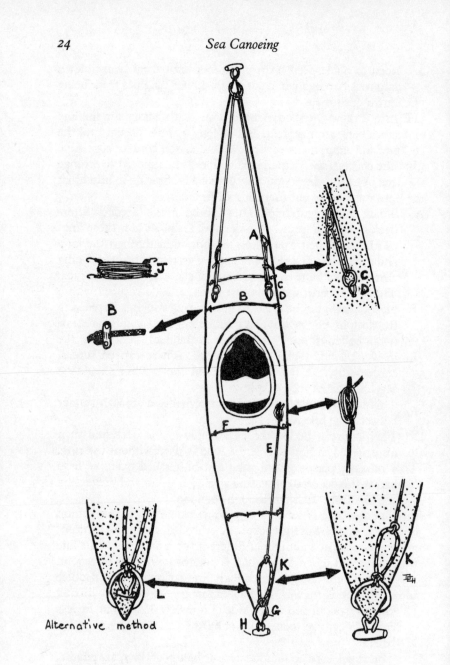

Figure 6. Deck lines (painters).

drip ring near the ferrule joint of the paddle prevents the metal parts from scraping the deck.

G. The spliced rope ring has the tow line looped through it.

H. The toggle uses a separate hole through the hull although it can be looped around and through the spliced rope ring similar to the manner in L.

J. After designing and trying a number of solid wave deflectors, I consider that probably the most satisfactory is a loose coil of rope, fixed to the shock cord fittings by very short car elastics that allow the rope to spring back as the wave strikes, thus absorbing the shock and dissipating the force in loose coils. This effectively stops the water from striking all the bits and pieces fastened on the foredeck in front of the cockpit only to be deflected in a multitude of different directions—into the eyes, up the nose and against the neck.

K. A loop of thick shock cord is introduced into the tow line to absorb the tremendous jerk which can occasionally be felt in heavy seas.

L. This is an alternative way of fixing shock cord to include the toggle on the existing rope ring.

Rudders

These undoubtedly help to maintain a course in awkward seas and to eliminate the need for tiring and frustrating corrective strokes. They seem to have been more popular for general sea canoeing in Scotland than in England.

Thin wire or nylon cord leads from the rudder mechanism in through the deck either behind or to the side of the cockpit and is then connected to foot-operated pedals or to a T bar, both worked in the same way by knocking the bar from one side to the other with the feet.

Although rudders are a considerable help, they bring with them added problems:

1. Any one of the deep water rescues can damage the wires or the actual rudder mechanism.

2. Seal landings and especially seal launchings are made very difficult.

3. Towing is almost impossible.

4. In my experience, when rudders break or bend they usually do so at a time and in a position that make paddling ten times worse than it would be with no rudder at all.

Packing

When packing the canoe, try to keep all the heavy gear near the centre, away from the bow and stern. If the weight is at the extremities, some inertia will be produced when the canoe is turning.

A certain amount of care must be exercised in balancing the canoe by distributing the weight fore and aft. But it is surprising how little the trim of the canoe is affected by quite heavy loads.

A small space should be left behind the seat for emergency gear (first aid, repair kit, exposure bag and any odd items of clothing needed during the trip). These should all be held in place by shock cord stretched across the canoe and attached to small loops glassed onto the inside of the hull.

One of the biggest boons when packing the fore end is a swing-out fail-safe footrest. This saves a great deal of time and the use of strenuous bodily contortions.

All bags should be secured with either rope or shock cord or else stored behind inflated tailored air bags, so that they will not float out in the event of a capsize.

MODERN SEA KAYAKS

In tracing the history of the modern sea canoe, it becomes apparent that many different types of boats have been used, few of which have been purpose built. Most men who explored the delights of sea canoeing made 'one-off' canoes, the design being duplicated only for a few friends. Others paddled standard canoes currently in use, sometimes adapting them.

The Tyne Single canoe was very popular and so were some of the longer boats designed by Percy Blandford. The Klepper company produced the famous Arius with inflatable airsponsons alongside the gunwales making it unsinkable and leaving all the room inside for equipment. The double version of this design gained immortality after the Atlantic crossings by Captain Romer in 1928 and Hannes Lindemann in 1956.

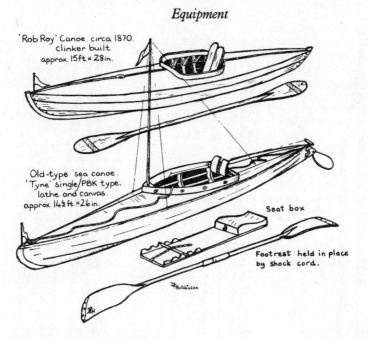

Figure 7. Early sea kayaks.

The Rob Roy canoe, popularised by John McGregor, was often used for sea and estuary work and even surfing. It was built of overlapping wooden planks which were fastened to the steam-bent frames by copper nails clinched home in the traditional clinker-built rowing boat style. These boats were very strong and heavy; whether they were true canoes in that they could be portaged by the one-man crew is debatable. Note the unfeathered paddle blades, the cockpit coaming with no provision for a spray cover, the hole in the foredeck to take a mast for a small lugsail and the rather bizarre backrest. When under sail the paddle was used to steer.*

In the old type of sea kayak, the bow and stern were reinforced by a brass strip extending about 1 ft. along the bottom of the keel. The canoes were made either rigid or with a folding frame and skin which fitted into 2 bags, one about 5 ft. long for the frame, the other rather more square for the rubber-proofed canvas hull covering. The large press-studs illustrated around the cockpit coaming were used to secure the spray cover until it was found that they corroded and filled with sand, becoming quite useless.

*O. J. Cock, *A Short History of Canoeing in Britain*, BCU 1974.

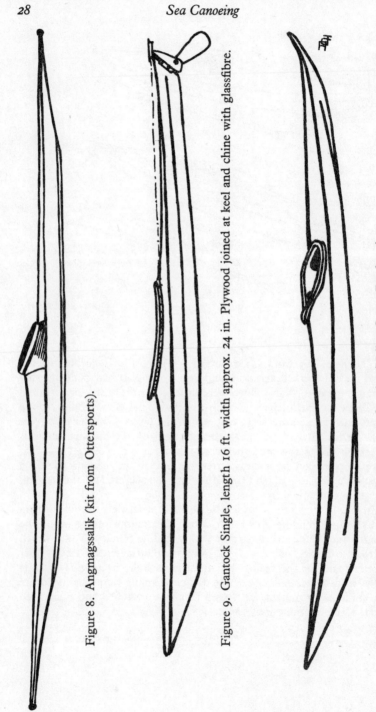

Figure 8. Angmagssalik (kit from Ottersports).

Figure 9. Gantock Single, length 16 ft. width approx. 24 in. Plywood joined at keel and chine with glassfibre.

Figure 10. Anas Acuta, length approx. 17 ft. 3 in. (Valley Canoe Products).

Some firms started producing boats modelled very closely on Eskimo designs, but which demanded a very high degree of skill from the men paddling them. The Tyne Greenland, the Ottersports Angmagssalik (Figure 8) and the Klepper Eskimo were all this type.

Scotland with its wild, lonely offshore islands has been a home of sea canoeing for many years and has consistently produced many good designs. In the 1930s John Marshal designed the Queensferry, which was still popular in 1955. Boats in this range were about 14 ft. long with a beam of 30 in. The hull was of hard chine form, the heavy frame covered in canvas. Another popular boat at that time was the Loch Lomond, designed by H.A.Y. Stevenson. This was light in build with more stringers (i.e. longitudinal laths) giving a rounder hull form. A couple of years later came the Clyde Single, a graceful kayak designed by Joe Reid, 16 ft. 3 in. long by 25½ in. wide; it was a hard chine form with a short V. Duncan Winning designed the Kempock and Cloch single kayaks; then he and Joe Reid combined to produce R. and W. Canoe Plans, the first being the 16 ft. long Gantock Single (Figure 9). Ken Taylor, a fellow club member with Duncan Winning, brought a kayak back from Greenland that inspired Andrew Carnuff to produce the Skua, approximately 15½ ft. long by 23 in. wide, which was then reproduced in glassfibre by John Flett, eventually to find its way into the fields of education and coaching. The Ken Taylor kayak from Igdlorssuit was also to have its influence on canoe design much farther field. Duncan Winning sent the drawings of this boat down to Geoff Blackford on the south coast of England. When Geoff later produced his Anas Acuta sea kayak he succeeded in combining the hull design of the Ken Taylor kayak with a modified deck specifically aimed at accommodating a European adult.

In recent years a number of sea boats of poor design have been produced commercially. Some had excess windage, some would not keep straight, some were just too tippy for words. All have fallen by the wayside.

As I write, the Gaybo Esky and Atlantic and Trylon Sea-hawk look seaworthy and appear to be well-designed craft, although they have not been tested by enough advanced sea canoeists to give a thorough apparaisal of their performance.

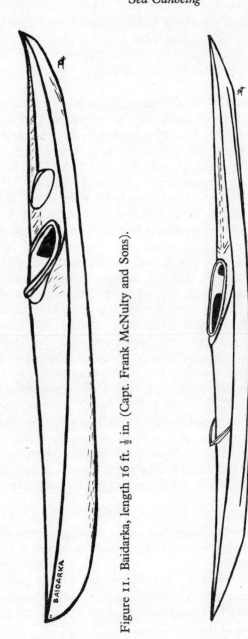

Figure 11. Baidarka, length 16 ft. $\frac{1}{2}$ in. (Capt. Frank McNulty and Sons).

Figure 12. Lindisfarne (Northern Kayaks).

Although I have paddled almost all the known sea kayaks, the boats I feel I have tested sufficiently thoroughly to report on in detail are the Anas Acuta, the Lindisfarne and one of my own design, the Baidarka. All three have been designed with comfort and stability in mind and all take into consideration the build and stature of European men. I have paddled these three in all conditions and through personal experience I consider them the best of the Eskimo-type kayaks.

Anas Acuta

Named from the Latin for pin tail, this boat is an Eskimo kayak in the true tradition, having a chine hull and a long, straight, elegant stem and a turned-up stern (Figure 10). About 17 ft. 3 in. in length, it is a stable, true rough-water sea boat. With a faithful band of devotees amongst the more advanced sea canoeists, its movements are predictable and it is very easy to roll. Large quantities of camping gear can be carried inside as well as on the rear deck without any appreciable alteration in freeboard. It has a fine narrow bow with a very long stem that tends to make the boat plunge slightly in even moderate head seas. The boat also tends to pivot on a point about a foot forward of the cockpit so that although it turns easily in high winds there is some broaching in a quartering sea. I adapted mine to overcome this by moulding a glassfibre skeg onto the underside of the hull at the rear.

Baidarka

In this boat (Figure 11) I attempted to retain the best qualities from an earlier design of mine while making modifications influenced by the best qualities of the Anas Acuta.

Approximately 16 ft. $\frac{1}{2}$ in. long, it has stability, room, elegance, comfort and ease of turning together with a round hull shape giving it great speed. The fullness at bow and stern prevents it from digging into waves. Its curved stem enables the powerful bow to slice through waves throwing much of the water sideways. It has a swing-out fail-safe footrest, allowing large amounts of camping gear forward while the rear deck is shaped to accommodate a large hatch, giving access to the area underneath. This

hatch coupled with a watertight bulkhead about a foot back from
the cockpit makes the boat ideal for storage of quite bulky equipment. There is about a cubic foot of space behind the cockpit
giving room for emergency equipment needed on long trips. The
boat runs straight and true even in a quartering sea, yet although
the keel is straight, the ease with which it turns in winds of Force 8
is remarkable. The cockpit coaming is large and watertight, while
knee grooves are situated on the foredeck directly in front of and
to the sides of the cockpit.

Lindisfarne

This good seaworthy canoe, about 16 ft. 2 in. long, is an Eskimo
kayak with a chine hull (Figure 12). The rear deck is very flat
along its length right to the low stern. Strengthening grooves run
across and down its length. A small V shaped wavebreak, incorporated in the foredeck halfway along its length, serves as a
convenient jointing place for the two parts of the upper deck, one
piece of which extends from the stern to the middle of the foredeck, the other piece going on from there to the bow.

The rather low bow causes the boat to plunge so that although
it is strongly built and handles well in rough water, the trip can be
a wet one even in the mildest of head seas. As for the wavebreak, it
raises the same question as all wavebreaks: not whether it will
deflect the water that rushes along the deck but where it will
deflect it.

In a quartering sea the boat tends to broach but this can be
corrected to some extent by moulding or fitting a skeg aft.

SLALOM CANOE

This type of canoe is reasonably satisfactory for sea canoeing, but
remember that it is a slow craft tending to plane even at slow speed.
This means that it is almost useless in very fast tidal streams. Nor
is its bow meant to cope with sea waves. Its rockered hull was
originally designed for turning corners and tight manoeuvring so
that it is hardly suitable for straight running at sea.

A skeg (Figure 13) can be fitted to make the slalom run straight,
but as mentioned earlier in this chapter, remember that moving

the pivot point to the back in this way makes it almost impossible to turn the boat in a high wind. A seal landing becomes very difficult and seal launchings are almost impossible. A skeg can also foul your own fishing line or can catch on floating nets or lobster pot lines. Two firms, Valley Canoe Products Ltd. and P. & H. Fibreglass Products, have experimented successfully with a skeg which can be retracted in a recess the same shape as the skeg. A thin line sleeved in nylon leads from a point just behind the cockpit through the hull and through the top of the recess and is attached to the skeg. Pulling the small ring behind the cockpit raises or lowers the skeg as desired.

Although slalom canoes are quite roomy, providing inner storage space for camping gear, the steep decks are not very suited to carrying spare paddles and excess equipment.

PADDLES

When considering the viability of various paddle shapes, it must be remembered that when Rob Roy popularised the use of the canoe in Britain during Victorian times, it is probable that John McGregor based his paddle shape on the oar used at the time for

Figure 13. Slalom canoe fitted with detachable glassfibre skeg. Made by moulding over the canoe itself, which ensures a perfect fit, the skeg effectively provides a long fin under the hull at the stern to ensure straight running at sea and it helps in some way to convert the slalom canoe for sea use. Probably the best way to secure a skeg is by a loop of thick shock cord which fits into a hook just behind the cockpit. If the skeg tangles irrevocably with something it can always be released quickly and completely by the man in the cockpit. Some sort of flotation foam can be fixed to the skeg so that it will float if it becomes disconnected from the canoe, or if it is thrown into the water before a seal launching. The skeg can be left to float until the canoe has been slid off the rocks and been paddled over to it.

c

rowing. Because of this, canoeists have ever since found themselves obliged to use what is, in effect, a double-ended oar rather than a paddle designed specifically for the sea canoeist. Many people use the same type of paddle for sea touring as for surfing and inland water, but in the last few years, since the rise in popularity of the true Eskimo type kayak, various sea canoeists have adopted a longer, narrower blade, based on original Eskimo designs. Blades are feathered—that is, set at right angles to each other—so that the upper blade offers little wind resistance when pushed forward during the forward paddle stroke cycle.

Some paddles used by white-water and slalom canoeists have spoon or dished blades. These can be the expensive, hand-carved, one-piece type or the much cheaper type where glassfibre or wooden blades are secured into an aluminium tube covered with a PVC sleeve. For normal weather conditions these are satisfactory, but in extremely high winds and rough seas the upper blade can 'flutter' and twist when caught by the wind, and if the hands are numb with cold this can cause an incorrect presentation or slice with the lower blade that will perhaps lead to an unwelcome capsize.

Flat wooden blades can be bought in kit form and supplied with an aluminium loom. By using a vice to flatten the loom in a position where the hand normally goes and at right angles to the nearest blade, and by then rubbing the slippery PVC with wire wool or scouring powder, a positive grip is ensured even in bad conditions. The forward propulsion, however, is not as efficient as with spoon blades.

As a general rule, if you stand behind the paddle with its bottom blade next to your toes and reach up, and if you can just hook your fingers over the top of the blade without stretching your body or your arm, then the length is about right for you (Figure 14). The same length is right for surfing and white water. True sea-touring paddles can be longer, by anything from 9 in. to 1 ft.

The area of a normal blade is about 690 sq. cm. If this is placed at the end of a longer loom, the strain at the joint between the blade and the loom is increased. But if, while preserving this area of 690 sq. cm. the blade is shaped longer and much narrower, then, even if the loom is no longer, the stroke is lengthened. Because the water pressure is much more gradual on the blade as

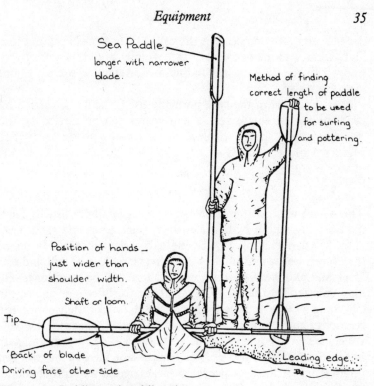

Sea Paddle, longer with narrower blade.

Method of finding correct length of paddle to be used for surfing and pottering.

Position of hands – just wider than shoulder width.

Shaft or loom.

Tip.

'Back' of blade
Driving face other side

Leading edge.

Figure 14. Paddles and paddle grip.

it is pulled through the water, it is rather like paddling in low gear. The propulsion is the same but the effort seems less, and with the increase in length, the upper blade is therefore lower during the stroke, presenting not only a better angle to any wind there might be but also a thinner shape offering less resistance. (See Figure 20.)

In cold weather, rubber drip rings prevent the hands being numbed by the constant trickle of cold water. All paddles should be painted in bright colours, preferably fluorescent, so that they can help the canoeist to be easily seen on the water.

During rescues, your paddle can be held in a paddle park, which is usually attached to one of the elastics on the foredeck. Made from the bracket which is normally screwed up in a cupboard to hold the handle of a broom or spade, mine is covered with polythene petrol tube to save damaging the PVC-covered loom. Using a paddle park is safer than pushing the paddle through one of the

deck elastics, in which case if the canoe were to swing round in a
high wind and then capsize, the paddle would be effectively
trapped in the deck elastic, foiling any attempt to roll up again.
(See Figure 17.)

Spare paddles, of the type normally used, should be carried by
those venturing out to sea. These spares can be carried on the
rear deck, held firmly in place by elasticated shock cord. (See
Figures 6 and 17.)

CLOTHING

The novice who has never had the benefit of advice usually faces
sea canoeing with a bathing costume, shirt, jeans and sandshoes.
After his first chilling capsize, he will seek guidance. He might
then buy a wet-suit as used by skin divers. At first he will find this
ideal, and all his swims and tows to shore will be warm ones. He
may then try for the BCU's Proficiency Certificate or one of the
Coaching awards and discover that the sleeves of the wet-suit are
restrictive and chafe under his armpits while he paddles the trips
which are pre-requisite to the test. Encouraged by the already
initiated, he cuts the sleeves from his wet-suit, wears a thin woollen
pullover under the now sleeveless jacket, and a waterproof anorak
or a special waterproof smock with a Velcro fastening and man-
darin collar over the top of the whole lot. Waterproof cuffs can
be made from the old cut-off sleeves, ensuring that tantalising
little dribbles of cold water don't eventually form a pool in the
elbow, only to rush under the warm armpit when the paddle is
raised higher than normal. Complete with wet-suit bootees,
sandals, socks or a combination of all three in any order—e.g.
socks under wet-suit boots or over them to stop slipping—our
intrepid hero is now ready. He can comfortably paddle long trips,
can be happy about jumping into the water to take part in any
necessary rescues, and can also surf in the knowledge that if
anything, he might overheat rather than freeze.

Once an advanced standard has been reached and surfing is not
contemplated as part of the trip, paddlers seem to turn a full circle
in their ideas of clothing, and revert to warm, baggy, comfortable
trousers, sloppy woollen pullovers over comfortable shirts. All this
covered with waterproof trousers and the usual anorak, with the

close-fitting neck and slipover cuffs at the wrists, makes a good combination. When the canoeist is sealed in with a tightly fitting spray cover, this outfit makes even Eskimo rolling a not-too-chilling experience. Footwear can consist of thick woollen socks and loose-fitting gumboots cut down very short. The gumboots really can be kicked off in the water quite easily if the need arises, especially when the canoeist is supported by a buoyancy aid or lifejacket. The headgear of advanced sea paddlers enters the world of the bizarre, including bush-hats, straw hats, battered trilbys, woolly pompom hats and fancy sailing caps, all usually of a size which will enable them to be placed, if conditions turn sour, over a neoprene hood with earholes cut out.

Instead of the baggy pants, wet-suit trousers can still be worn as part of the combination, but a decision has to be made by the advanced sea canoeist. In order to be prepared for an unlikely capsize, is he to paddle stinking, sweating, steaming and prickling in rubber equipment like an out-of-work frogman? Or is he to dress like a sensibly turned-out hill walker, depending more on his skill and expertise to keep dry, and meet the freezing rescue when the time comes—if ever.

During the cold winter months, when the water and air temperatures are at their lowest, the canoeist's most important consideration is loss of body heat through immersion in cold water or through chilling exposure to wind or by a combination of both. At such times, wool, which generates heat when wet, is probably the ideal material for an undergarment but it can be a little irritating next to the skin. The Damart Company manufacture thermal underwear of a man-made fibre which is extremely warm as well as comfortable. I have worn one of their Polojama suits as an undergarment, rolling at sea during winter months in an air temperature as low as 38°F. in winds of Force 8. Its comfort derives from the fact that it is so fine and lightweight, and as a piece of emergency equipment it dries easily and packs into an extremely small space.

If the arms and body are warm, the hands usually warm up after a short while. However, if conditions are very cold, thin rubber gloves over woollen gloves can be used, or some of the excellent thin neoprene or specially treated leather ones used for diving and sailing.

BASIC EQUIPMENT

Lifejackets

It will be noticed that the lifejacket in Figure 15 when worn has most of its buoyancy at the front with a buoyant halter around the neck. It is a two-stage lifejacket; that is, it has a piece of sponge enclosed in a thin polythene bag inside the main front compartment, and this combined with a piece of sponge inside the neck halter gives an 'inherent' buoyancy of about 14 lb. whilst uninflated for the first stage. The second stage, after the lifejacket has been inflated, gives a buoyancy of more than 35 lb. which can twist the body of a helpless man around from the face-down position to a survival position of about 45° to the water with mouth and nose clear *under normal conditions*. The lifejacket is worn deflated in the canoe and blown up only in case of emergency *in the water*. If, in the event of a capsize in very cold water, you should lose consciousness through hypothermia, an *inflated* lifejacket will keep your face out of the water, so long as the sea is not too rough, thus increasing your chances of survival.

As a member of the British Canoe Union's Coaching Scheme I advise all those about to embark on the sport of canoeing to wear a BSI 3595 lifejacket. However, certain other aspects must be taken into consideration. The lifejacket must be blown up before it becomes a true lifejacket. Until then, it is just a rather inefficient buoyancy aid. People tend to chew and destroy the deflation tongue. The lifejacket gives no thermal or any other type of protection to the back. One has a choice of tying either a quick-release knot that always comes undone at the wrong time or a knot that is difficult to untie quickly. Buckles were tried and then for some reason rejected. The bottom of the waterproof outer case tends to wear and should be worn with a special cover to extend, possibly even double, the life of the main casing. If the outer casing is ripped and the inner polythene envelope is also damaged, the inner sponge, which is not closed-cell, soaks up the water, forming a millstone round the neck of the canoeist.

I was carried from the sea one cold Sunday in December 1966 while training a group of lifeguards in surf techniques. I 'drowned' into unconsciousness over a period of about 15 minutes out in the surf. Exhausted, breathless and confused, I was prevented from

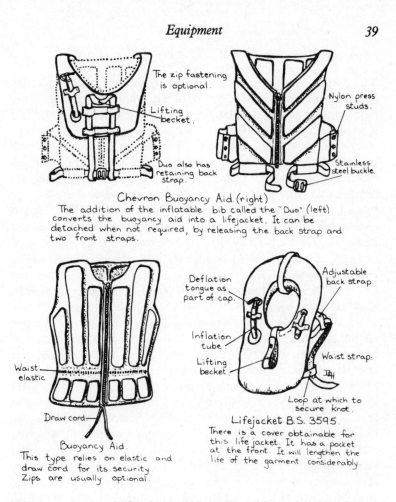

The zip fastening is optional.

Lifting becket.

Nylon press studs.

Duo also has retaining back strap.

Stainless steel buckle.

Chevron Buoyancy Aid. (right)
The addition of the inflatable bib called the "Duo" (left) converts the buoyancy aid into a lifejacket. It can be detached when not required, by releasing the back strap and two front straps.

Deflation tongue as part of cap.

Adjustable back strap.

Inflation tube.

Lifting becket.

Waist strap.

Waist elastic

Loop at which to secure knot.

Draw cord

Lifejacket B.S. 3595.
There is a cover obtainable for this life jacket. It has a pocket at the front. It will lengthen the life of the garment considerably.

Buoyancy Aid.
This type relies on elastic and draw cord for its security. Zips are usually optional.

Figure 15. Types of lifejackets and buoyancy aids used in canoeing.

turning my head to one side to vomit by the same lifejacket which kept bringing me to the surface in the huge tumbling stormwater waves. By the time I used my failing energy to twist sideways in order to clear my blocked throat and suck another breath, the next wave sent me choking underneath. I must have blacked out several times until I awoke standing against a wet wall, I thought. It was no wall, but the sand by the water's edge where I had been dragged after being taken from the water.

Buoyancy Aids

The thing to remember about a buoyancy aid is that it will not turn
and hold the body in the lean-back survival position, but rather
hold it in an upright position, allowing the head to loll forwards if
it wants.

The majority of the advanced sea canoeists I associate with all
wear buoyancy aids of one type or another. I have worn both types
illustrated in Figure 15 and found them satisfactory. They are
comfortable to wear, help keep the body warm and are easy to
swim in. Any zips are the heavy diving-suit type. The foam is
closed-cell, and they can also serve as a seat or pillow without any
damage to their efficiency. In lifeguard and in beach rescue work
as an aid to swimming, I consider them invaluable. I once had to
enter the water amongst rocks in surf, and although I damaged
legs and arms, the buoyancy aid protected my spine and chest.
Wearing anything else I would have been badly injured.

A recent additional development to the Chevron buoyancy aid is
an inflatable halter (Figure 15). The bib front of the halter is
fastened by two webbing straps to the waistbelt of the buoyancy aid
and the collar at the back is secured in the same manner to the rear
of the waistbelt. The inflation tube is situated on the right-hand
side. To avoid bulkiness on the shoulder, the flat deflated jacket
is folded back upon itself and secured by Velcro. When blown up,
the whole halter inflates and the Velcro springs open, allowing the
folded parts to open out as they fill with air, and to form a collar
around the neck and back of the head. The additional buoyancy
thus converts what was already an excellent buoyancy aid into a
true lifejacket, conforming to the requirements of the British
Standards Institute. The two parts can be bought separately or
bought together as the Chevron Duo. For expedition purposes, a
large 'Velcro'-sealed pocket incorporated in the back of the
buoyancy aid could be used to carry the 'Duo' attachment or perhaps a self-inflating (CO_2) lifejacket. The pocket should be in a
position where the wearer can reach and open it by means of a
looped release-tab. This would make the life-jacket accessible even
when the wearer is in the water.

In this book most of the illustrations show people wearing
something resembling a buoyancy aid, although it could well be a

type of lifejacket. As I write, the whole concept of the lifejacket is in a state of flux as to shape, size and type, so today's description may not apply to tomorrow's lifejacket. The choice of lifejacket or buoyancy aid for the advanced sea canoeist will remain a personal one. But it is a choice only of type—one kind or another *must* be worn at sea *always*.

Waterproof bags and containers

'The only thing that's really waterproof is a frog's ear.' Remember this when you consider protecting anything from the penetrating efforts of salt water.

As with many of the small items of equipment, the best and most satisfying results come from either improvising or making your own waterproof bags and containers. I made my bags from

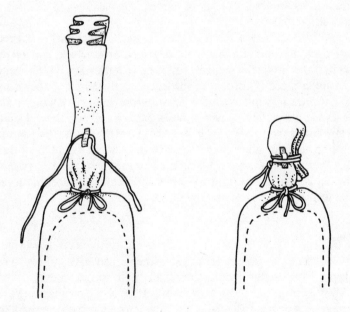

Figure 16. Method of securing the necks of waterproof bags.

army ground sheet, with stitched seams and with longs strips of the same material glued onto the inside to make the seams waterproof. Equipment is sealed inside a polythene bag and then placed in the main waterproof bag and secured as in Figure 16. Polythene bags are not suitable on their own as they tend to crack and split when tied or squeezed into tight places.

People sometimes complain that access is difficult when loading equipment into a canoe, especially behind the seat and under the back deck. When making your waterproof bags, take this into consideration. It doesn't matter, for instance, if your tent is in four different bags so long as they are the right shape and length to go into any awkward places. Indeed, many small bags are better than a few large ones as it is easier to balance the stowed gear and, of course, in the event of a capsize, all one's eggs are not in the same waterproof basket.

Waterproof screw-top containers are a big help, although sometimes they are a little too large to get past the seat and under the rear deck. A little petroleum jelly or grease on the top of the container helps to create a more waterproof seal when the lid is screwed down.

Some canoes have a hatch on the rear deck, which makes packing very easy. Remember that a little grease around the rim of the hatch, if it is a plastic one, helps to keep it watertight. Don't forget to fasten a piece of cord from the canoe to the hatch so that if the top happens to slip from your grasp while you are delving inside the canoe out at sea, it won't swell the contents of Davy Jones's locker and leave you with a gaping hole in your deck. Instead of a screw hatch, an aluminium 'Henderson' hatch could be fitted. This has a snap-down lid which incorporates a rubber washer. The lid is held down tight by means of a cam-type locking lever. It is probably the most watertight of all hatches.

Compass

Unlike dinghy sailors and yachtsmen, canoeists don't have compasses specially manufactured for their specific needs.

Most confidence is usually inspired by one's own handiwork. Armed with a dome-shaped car compass, or any small compass for that matter—it need not be waterproof—and a moulding kit of clear plastic so popular with children, it is possible with a little ingenuity to produce a compass which will take the shape of the deck exactly, which can have either lugs or a hole for straps or cord, which will be unbreakable and which will be easily seen.

If, however, one wishes to buy the readymade article, the Sestral Junior Compass has a dome shape and a gimbal to keep it horizontal at sea by allowing the compass to swing with the motion of the canoe. Unfortunately, these sometimes get in the way during rescues and can get damaged or lost.

Orienteering compasses are clear and easy to read. The Suunto from Finland is particularly good, the needle being slowed right down by the thick liquid filling. The course is easily set by means of a moving bezel, and the luminous pointer and course marks are easily seen at night. In the event of complicated island-hopping in bad visibility, it is advisable to have an orienteering compass hanging around the neck or at least somewhere handy so that it can be used in conjunction with the main compass on the deck when plotting the course from a chart.

For normal bad visibility paddling, I use a Suunto diving compass set onto a homemade base. Being a little shortsighted, I find the clear markings an advantage for both day and night paddling. The compass is kept on a string fastened to one of the deck elastics or sometimes to the loop on the release strap of my spray cover, so that in the event of my having to rescue someone I can either lay it on top of my spray cover or let it hang over the side in the water out of harm's way. Some neoprene spray covers can have a pocket glued on with a hole cut into it which allows the face of the compass to show through.

EMERGENCY EQUIPMENT

Even on short trips, emergency equipment should be carried inside the canoe where it can be reached in a hurry.

Repair Kit

The minimum repair kit has been said to be a roll of wide waterproof self-adhesive tape for patching the canoe. But as it is foolhardy to go to sea with the minimum amount of equipment,

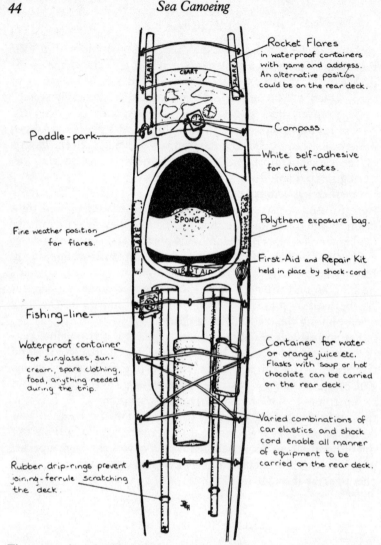

Rocket Flares in waterproof containers with name and address. An alternative position could be on the rear deck.

CHART

FLARES

Paddle-park.

Compass.

White self-adhesive for chart notes.

Fine weather position for flares.

FLARE

SPONGE

REPAIR STAID

EXPOSURE BAG

Polythene exposure bag.

First-Aid and Repair Kit held in place by shock-cord

Fishing-line.

Waterproof container for sunglasses, sun-cream, spare clothing, food, anything needed during the trip.

Container for water or orange juice etc. Flasks with soup or hot chocolate can be carried on the rear deck.

Varied combinations of car elastics and shock cord enable all manner of equipment to be carried on the rear deck.

Rubber drip-rings prevent joining-ferrule scratching the deck.

Figure 17. A typical deck layout. Each man will carry what he needs in a position where he can reach it. Apart from the items shown, the layout might also include a sun hat, sunglasses, a fishing spear, bait for a line, caught fish, a *waterproof* camera bag, even a set of deer antlers—on some Scottish islands stags run wild—in fact any bric-a-brac which one may carry on the deck rather than inside the boat itself.

When you have your canoe fitted out to suit yourself and have tied everything onto small safety lines, take your boat out into small surf. Play about letting the waves break over your deck for about 10 minutes; then go back to shore and check to see if what was on the deck to start with is *still* there, and if what was placed in the safety of containers and waterproof bags is *still* dry. If all *is* still there *and* still dry, congratulate yourself.

consider some of the things you may have to do either for yourself or for some other unfortunate canoeist:

Join spray cover elastic by crimping pieces of wire with pliers

Patch a buoyancy bag with a piece of PVC (PVC glue) or a lifejacket with a piece of rubberised cloth (Evostick)

Repair a hole in a spray cover

Stitch something together (waxed thread and needles with a sailor's palm)

Dry your canoe or stick tape onto it

Clean the surface (Acetone)

Require some string, cord or wire

Burn the fraying end of a splice (waterproof matches/lighter) or light a stove

Open a tin (small ex-WD type opener—the best)

Make a phone call or buy a pint and a pie for, say, four people

Need some toilet paper (kitchen roll is more substantial when damp)

Fasten something with a safety pin or tighten a screw

Cut something (scissors or a sharp knife)

Repair a hole in a wet-suit (carry a patch)

Repair a tent ('Awl-you-need' from Blacks of Greenock, Scotland) or a ground sheet

Need a pencil and paper or a spare set of tide tables.

First Aid

Just as the roll of tape is the minimum repair kit for the canoe, I suppose a roll of medicated plaster is a comparable repair kit for the human body. While canoeing I have been faced with the following small problems:

Scalding tea over knees and hands

Jellyfish or wasp and bee stings (Anthisan anti-histamine cream)

Burnt hands

Fish hooks in fingers (pliers from repair kit)

Headaches and toothache

Sickness and nausea

Both mild and severe glass-bottle cuts to the feet

Midges and seeds in the eyes or spines from sea urchins embedded in fingers

Severe sunburn
Splinter of glassfibre up fingernail
Dislocated shoulder (lifejacket can be fastened under the
    arm for support)
Damaged ribs or pelvis
Severely cut hands
Drowning and cardiac arrest
Diabetic coma
Mild exposure and severe hypothermia
Severe chest cramp
Exhaustion and fear
A sprained ankle
Multiple injuries from a cliff fall

Accidents are those unexpected things which perhaps happen only once. A member of one party caught her head on a fish hook which had been left dangling over the water. A man at the end of a canoe was playfully trying to capsize it in a swimming pool, unaware that his noseclip was hanging through the sternloop. The man in the canoe chose just then to demonstrate how fast he could roll round and round. Try explaining this kind of strangulation to a coroner.

Flares

If you are in trouble—real trouble—you want to be seen to be in trouble easily—and quickly.

All the hand flares in the world are useless if the people on shore are fastening shoe-laces or walking head down into the wind and rain. You must make them *turn round and look*. Your first signal, therefore, must be audible as well as visual. I carry two Pains Wessex Yachtshutes for this purpose. These fire a rocket or star shell into the air to approximately 1000 ft.; a grenade then explodes and a bright red flare floats slowly to the ground giving people plenty of time to see it. Sometimes called a Maroon, this is one of the international signals of distress. Unless visibility is bad or you are a long way out to sea, the Maroon will probably also pinpoint your position, especially if your canoe is painted in bright colours. But carry hand flares too. These will help rescuers locate your position in bad visibility, especially if you have drifted a long way since sending up the star shell. I also carry three 2-star red flares. Not the exploding type, they send two bright red flares high into the air, with about a 5-second pause between.

Unfortunately, if your pyrotechnics don't work through contact with salt water, the manufacturers won't accept responsibility, and the polythene bags they are wrapped in cannot be trusted. Rather sad when one considers they are for use at sea. I carry my small flares separately in long aluminium screw-top containers within reach on the deck. I have protected even the largest para-chute flares by making special containers out of glassfibre, using a piece of pipe as a former. I have also seen very effective containers made from plumbers' plastic waste-pipe.

Pockets stitched to your personal buoyancy are an ideal place for carrying flares on your person, but it must be remembered that in this position they can be badly affected by the action of the salt water. It is quite pointless having your flares packed away inside the canoe. When you *need* them, the *last* thing you'll want to do is to remove your spray cover or dig deep down into your equipment.

There are a number of electronic safety devices which could be included in the emergency equipment. The SARBE Flotation Distress Beacon made by Burndept Electronics Ltd. is one which floats, is self-righting and transmits on civil and military distress frequencies. The SARBE 5 is a hand-held unit that transmits both distress signals and speech.

For very long open-sea expeditions, where the risk of trouble is ever-present and sleep is impossible, each man could well carry a self-inflating rubber dinghy in an accessible position on the rear deck, in some kind of quick-release protective case. Room to accommodate this could be made by moving the spare paddles much nearer the stern.

A Very pistol might be an additional useful piece of equipment. Because this would not float, it would be advisable to secure it by a lanyard. Cartridges in assorted colours should be kept handy. The possession of a Very pistol requires a firearms certificate.

An essential piece of emergency equipment is the exposure bag, a polythene bag, approximately 6 ft. by 3 ft., used to protect hypo-thermia cases from wind and cold. Their usual bright orange colour also makes them helpful in rescue spotting.

AUXILIARY EQUIPMENT

The Inner Man

Even on short trips take a hot sweet drink of some sort in a thermos flask. The sugar will help to restore your blood sugar level after strenuous activity and remember that if you make it with powdered milk, the drink will stay hot much longer. Protect your flask with some padding taped on or slipped over the outside; flasks never seem to last long otherwise. Some people prefer to take a small stove and have the hot drink or soup fresh; it all depends on personal fancy.

Emergency food may lie in the container for some time so choose something that doesn't go off—barley sugar, glucose sweets or the eternal Mars bar. Health food shops sell blocks of concentrated compressed fruit and vegetable compounds which last a long time and are very tasty as well as filling. Mountaineering shops also usually carry a good line in emergency and dried food.

Food and drink needed for the trip can be carried on the rear deck or inside the canoe, but if *on* the rear deck it means that if you wish, you can keep picking as you get hungry and have a quick gulp of warm orange juice as your thirst increases. However if you want the drink to stay cool and your chocolate biscuits to look like biscuits, not like some disgusting dark-brown soup, under the deck is the place for them.

Radio

For short one-day paddles, a radio is rather pointless, but for canoe camping, listening to the weather forecast for your area *can* be helpful. One does not necessarily have to choose the smallest radio in the world for canoeing. Space is not usually so limited, and it is quite possible to find oneself in a mountainous position where reception on a miniature radio is rather restricted.

Ensure that your piece of oriental electronics is well protected from water and is also *well padded*! Trying two or three Eskimo rolls or even executing a normal deep water rescue with the radio rattling round unprotected inside the canoe will not exactly enhance the general performance or improve the reception of your radio.

One last important warning:

KEEP THE RADIO AWAY FROM YOUR COMPASS

Waterproof Torch

This is just what it says, except that some torches are only 'water resistant' and hardly suitable for having water constantly breaking over them, let alone for being dropped into water. The type obtainable from diving shops, if not too large and heavy, can be taped to your helmet and used for night paddling, enabling you to work at the chart or compass without a break in your paddling. It is surprising how the luminosity of your compass will fade unless you keep giving it a flash from your torch to liven it up every now and then. I find a caver's headlamp ideal for this purpose. It dispenses with the need for a helmet and is much lighter to wear, leaving the torch on deck free for other things such as letting other water users know your position.

Sunglasses

Paddling directly into the sun not only can affect your view ahead, but it can also give you a severe headache. When not in use, sunglasses can be either worn around the neck on a cord or tucked under the deck elastics, in a plastic case perhaps.

The Eskimos use a solid, filled-in type of eye shield with thin slits cut out for each eye, allowing only a limited amount of sunlight to enter. I have experimented with this type of protection by filing a narrow slot in industrial protective spectacles and then painting them matt-black, and I have found them very satisfactory.

Watch

You'll need a watch to time trips or work out the tides if nothing else, and it must be waterproof. An expanding strap is useful so that the watch can be worn over neoprene cuffs. There was a time when a good waterproof watch cost a fortune. However, these days a good one can be had very reasonably.

D

Whistle

All good lifejackets seem to be supplied with a whistle, and they seem to be a wonderful toy for leaders who love audible signals. Two short blasts: 'Come to me'; one long: 'Stay where you are'; three blasts: 'Raft up and wait for me' . . . and so it goes. Each man seems to have his own system, which, combined with one hand held up, waved side to side, or the paddle held above the head, makes some canoe expedition leaders look like continental traffic policemen. When audible signals are *really needed* it is usually windy, and unless the people for whom your blast is intended are downwind—they'll probably never hear it anyway. Instead you will just have to paddle very fast and catch them up. As for an exhausted man trying to blow a whistle in the water to attract attention, I think that if he is within whistle range he'll probably be seen anyway.

It may seem ludicrous to dwell upon the merits of the pea operated and non-pea operated whistle. Lifejackets are fitted out with the non-pea type, which gives a low tone rather like a policeman's whistle, while the pea operated whistle gives a shrill piercing blast familiar to all school playgrounds. The pea operated type is ideal for leaders and instructors who wish to control large groups from the vantage point of the beach. Unfortunately, unless the pea is of the non-perishable, non-water-logging type, you'll soon find yourself blowing through noiseless pulp.

Learn to whistle by pursing the lips. It carries just as far if not farther than an ordinary whistle, and can be done while you are paddling because you don't have to take your hand off the paddle to do it.

Nose Clip

This very important piece of equipment consists simply of a steel or plastic spring which holds and presses two rubber disc-shaped pads against both sides of the nose. Before condemning it as being only for beginners, bear in mind that without doubt in some cases sudden death has been caused by water being *driven up* the nose. This has either slowed or arrested the heart through a reflex action involving the vagus nerve.* Capsizing a canoe is not like diving into water; the forces and pressures are different, and if a man pauses upside down while rolling, the pressure is sustained, and the sudden rush of water up the nose can be very painful.

When novices are doing their initial capsize or training for rolling, the nose clip can protect the canoeist from a great deal of discomfort and give him time, when upside down, to think of the more important aspects of what he is doing. During surf acrobatics or even while learning to surf, capsizes may come with some violence, without time to take that necessary quick intake of air. If a nose clip is worn and if the mouth is kept shut, this will stop an involuntary and dangerous inhalation of water through the nose.

Folding Canoe Trolley

The folding canoe trolley, an oft neglected piece of equipment, can be made from a pair of small pram-like wheels attached to a folding wooden cradle, which has webbing straps allowing it to be fixed under the fore end of a kayak. It enables the canoe, fully packed with camping gear, to be perambulated rather than portaged across long distances from loch to loch or bay to bay, perhaps avoiding dangerous headlands. If one is forced to make an unwanted landing, the trolley is readily available to take all equipment to a different launching place, perhaps a number of miles away. When not in use it folds up, the wheels detach and it can be packed either on or under the deck.

*W. R. Keatinge, *Survival in Cold Water*, Blackwell Scientific Publishers, 1969.

2
Technique

In the basic paddle grip (Figure 14) you will notice the hands are only a little wider apart than the shoulders. In very cold weather the hands can effectively be kept dry by placing them even closer together, while in a high wind the hands can be held farther apart as for inland white-water paddling, where the arms are at right angles to the paddle loom when it is held up and placed touching the top of the head.

BASIC TECHNIQUES

Launching from a Flat Beach

This is usually quite easy, especially in a glassfibre canoe. Watch and judge how far the waves swill up the beach, choose a lull, climb into the cockpit and position yourself while the canoe rests on the sand, then secure the spray cover. The next large wave washing up the beach should put enough water under your hull to enable you to push off and paddle through the waves. When you meet the waves coming towards you do not raise your paddle in the air above your head, but rather keep on paddling straight through with your head down.

On a very flat beach it is possible to sit in the canoe ready for the big moment and find that the sea appears to have receded. There are some who advocate knuckling down towards the water using a hand on either side of the canoe. Unfortunately my arms are rather short and when I clench my fists, the knuckles do not reach the

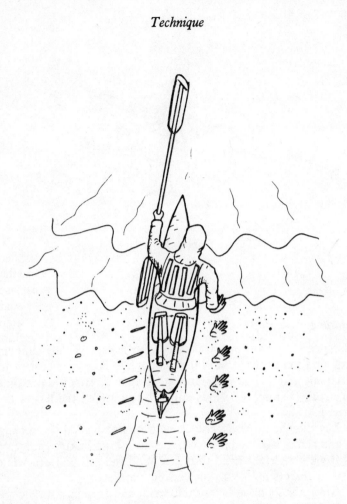

Figure 18. Launching from a flat beach: ' a trail in the sand reminiscent
of a one-armed mermaid. . . .'

sand together. I prefer to use an upright paddle on one side and,
by leaning over, to put my flat palm on the other. Then by a series
of lifts and ungainly forward jerks, the canoeist makes his awkward
way to the water's edge, leaving a trail in the sand reminiscent of a
one-armed mermaid. (Figure 18).

Figure 19. Method of entry from rocks or landing stage.

Launching from Rocks

Taking care not to slip as you carry your kayak over the slippery rocks, find some water that is deep enough to float your boat clear. Watch out that the surge doesn't lift it up and settle it down on a sharp rock (Figure 19). Now, suppose you are on the left of the canoe.

1. Lay the paddle across the canoe deck just behind the cockpit and across a convenient rock, thus forming a linking bridge.
2. Hook your right hand thumb around the paddle loom while your fingers hold onto the cockpit rim.
3. Grasp the loom with your left hand, and keeping your weight mainly on this hand, sit on the loom almost where it meets the canoe deck, and lift your legs into the cockpit.
4. Transfer the paddle to the front of the cockpit or a paddle park and adjust the spray cover.

When disembarking do this in reverse. But as you leave the canoe and stand up, remember to hook your paddle into the cockpit in case the kayak drifts away. Many a good man has prized his stiff limbs from the cockpit, straightened up and stretched with relief, only to turn round to see his boat bobbing in about 5 ft. of water just out of paddle reach.

Forward Paddling Stroke

ORTHODOX METHOD This stroke has only a limited use in sea canoeing. As seen in Figure 20, the man leans aggressively forward. His back is unsupported. His left arm pushes forwards and will finish up straight out at maximum stretch with his left shoulder twisted forward. During the stroke his left hand is relaxed, perhaps open, the fingers forward. His right arm pulls the paddle backwards, bringing the blade close to the hull.

Notice the height of the upper blade. This is a sure beam wind catcher, while the lower blade is purely propulsive, giving hardly any support in rough conditions.

SEA CANOEING METHOD The stroke may have to be continued over many hours, so it is as well to get comfortable. The feet should rest firmly on the footrest. For general touring most sea canoeists tend to keep their legs straight out, raising their knees and bracing them against the deck or roll bars only if conditions are rough or the possibility of a roll might be around the corner.

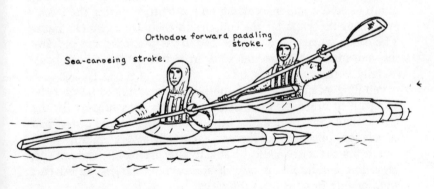

Figure 20. Forward paddling stroke. The sea paddle shown could be called a compromise between a modern paddle and the original Eskimo paddle. I adapted the measurements to suit a European adult's height and build. The blades, approximately $5\frac{1}{2}$ by $19\frac{1}{4}$ in., were fitted into a normal aluminium loom. These are the only paddles for serious sea work.

The back should be supported against the back of the cockpit coaming, or in some way to suit the individual. I personally find an inflated buoyancy bag with a polystyrene float jammed in front of it is ideal. Thus the lower half of the body is braced between the footrest and the backrest. The body is upright, *not leaning backwards*. Supporting the back solidly is directly opposed to inland white-water and competition techniques, where the back should be unrestricted.

As the man pulls back with his right arm he presses his right foot onto the footrest. The upper left arm pushing forward is quite relaxed; the fingers can even be open as in the orthodox forward stroke. Unlike the orthodox stroke, the paddle is placed farther out from the side of the canoe, thus giving the stroke a slight sweep rather than a downwards plunge. The upper blade presents a more acute and therefore more favourable angle to any beam wind, with hardly any likelihood of the paddle being snatched or twisted from the upper hand by the wind. Because the paddle action is lower it is less tiring on the arms and shoulders.

Opening and closing alternate hands during the stroke cycle allows fresh blood and oxygen to circulate into the muscles, thus preventing cramp and helping to keep the hands from becoming numb in cold weather. Pressing on the footrest during the stroke cycle does the same for the muscles in the feet, legs and thighs. The canoe when 'worn' by the paddler is propelled not only by the movement of the trunk and arms but by the whole body literally *to the tips of the toes*.

Paddling a canoe without a footrest, making it necessary for the occupant to brace with the thighs without a firm support for the feet, is inefficient from a propulsion point of view, and causes bad circulation, pins and needles and eventually severe cramp.

The sea canoeist should be able to alter his paddle style to suit prevailing conditions in case of approaching danger, an adverse wind or tide race, or need for speed.

Remember that when paddling with a following sea, the paddling effort is not constant (see Figure 62). As the wave passes underneath, the effort should be eased, starting to build up again when the canoe is in the trough and reaching its maximum when the canoe is on the face of the wave slope, then gradually easing again as the crest is reached and passes underneath the canoe.

In calm conditions a beginner to sea canoeing should be able to paddle 3 or 4 miles, some perhaps a little farther. Blisters may form inside the thumb but these eventually give way to hard skin, and men and women who at first find 4 to 5 miles an ordeal can, after a few months' practice, paddle 20 to 25 miles quite easily in calm conditions.

Proficiency standard canoeists should manage between 12 to 20 miles depending on such things as age and sex. Advanced paddlers should achieve much in excess of this. However, all these distances may be increased if a strong wind is favourable, or cut down to a couple of miles even for an advanced paddler if conditions are very bad.

Figure 21. Sweep turn stroke.

Sweep Turn Stroke

In Figure 21 the man is leaning forward and the blade is placed as far forwards as possible with the driving face of the blade outwards. As the body sweeps the straight arm out and back, the moving blade is angled slightly so that it planes as well as pushes and also supports the man when he leans over onto the bilge. The waterline is thus shortened and the canoe easier to turn. With rockered canoes, under calm conditions, the paddle can be held in the normal paddling position, but with long straight-keeled Eskimo-type kayaks or in a strong wind, the paddle can be held in a more extended position, by sliding the hands along the loom, giving a longer lever on one side.

In the reverse sweep the paddle is swept out from the back of the canoe towards the bow using the back of the blade.

Draw Stroke

Sea canoeing is not just paddling in a straight line. There will be many instances when the canoe will have to be moved sideways. The basic stroke is done while the canoe is standing still, not moving forwards.

Positioning the canoe for rescues must be done quickly as time spent in cold water can be dangerous, and it is the draw stroke which will do this quicker than anything else. Speed is also important for the Eskimo rescue, because although in this rescue the dangers from cold water are less, the patient may well be holding his breath.

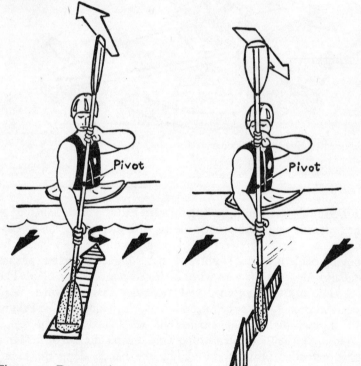

Figure 22. Draw stroke.

In Figure 22 the lower arm is pulling the driving face of the blade inwards during which time the blade stays at a constant depth in the water. The upper arm meanwhile pushes across, pivoting the paddle somewhere near the centre of the loom. Just before the blade is pulled under the hull, the paddle is quickly twisted in the direction of the small arrow through 90° and then sliced outwards into the starting position.

A common mistake is 'violining'. This occurs when the upper arm is moved up and down too much rather than being pushed across the body at about head height, and it causes the blade to slide up and down in the water with no 'drawing' power.

Whether the canoe is made to lean over on the stroke side as the paddle is drawn inwards depends on the hull shape. Curved hulls, like the slalom, draw best when the boat is upright. Eskimo kayaks with chine hulls and some sea boats with a ridge running along the centre of the hull seem to draw better when they lean over.

Support Strokes

SLAP SUPPORT   In part A of Figure 23 the man leans over *until he is off balance;* only then will he bring the paddle blade flat down smartly onto the surface of the water. As he feels his capsize halted by the paddle blade, he flicks the canoe upright as in B. Then with a twist of the wrist turning the blade through 90° he slices upwards, bringing the paddle out of the water.

PADDLE BRACE   Probably the most important sea canoeing technique, if we exclude an extremely strong forward paddling stroke, is the paddle brace. This is simply the ability to sit parallel to a breaking wave and stay upright. Once it is mastered, one's whole attitude towards bad weather, towards following and breaking seas out in deep water, is much more controlled and philosophical.

Sit sideways onto a small breaking wave (Figure 24). Your paddle should be extended outwards, the driving face downwards. As the wave breaks against the side of the canoe, knocking the boat shorewards, lean to seaward onto the paddle blade. This will be supported on top of the upsurge of power inside the wave, and you will move happily sideways in an upright position. *Never lean*

Figure 23. Slap support stroke. A shows the paddle blade in the extended position. B shows the paddle in the normal position. In B the best results are achieved by starting the down stroke slightly forwards of centre and then striking downwards and backwards. It is important that the paddler can do this stroke not only with the driving face of the blade as illustrated but also with the back of the blade, in case he finds himself in an unstable position while he is recovering his paddle from the rear of the canoe and moving it forwards.

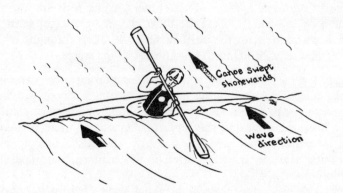

Figure 24. Paddle brace, small wave. The paddle is placed over and behind the breaking wave. If the wave was any larger the man would have to lean over even farther to absorb the shock as it breaks. Throughout the whole manoeuvre, the paddle is braced on top of the broken wave and the man is leaning upon it.

Figure 25. Paddle brace, large wave. The paddle is pushed into the face of the wave. Be prepared for the severe jerk!

shorewards away from the wave. If you do, you will capsize with great speed.

With practice, waves of quite gigantic proportions can be braced onto successfully. This is advanced surf technique. To brace into a very large wave (Figure 25), the paddle is pushed into the face of the wave as it breaks, with the driving side of the blade downwards, while the paddler leans right over into the wave. In some cases he can almost capsize into it. He must be prepared for a severe jerk on the arms at the initial impact, after which he is carried shorewards at great speed, holding his breath while the canoe bucks up and down in a welter of foam, noise and spray. The paddle is still extended seawards, supported on the upsurge inside the wave.

LOW BRACE This is of more use for the smaller, less violent type of wave. The support principal is the same as for the normal paddle brace except that the paddler leans on the *back of the blade*. As the canoe is swept shorewards it may start to swing round, pointing its bow in that direction. You will find that the paddle is now in the low telemark position and you can carry on your way, steering by this, or gently convert to a stern rudder, and by pushing outwards, put the canoe back parallel to the wave and into the low brace again.

Figure 26. Stern rudder turn, canoe moving forwards. The paddle blade is pushed away from the side. The canoe will turn on that side. If this is done whilst the canoe is running forwards on a wave, the paddler must be ready, as the canoe turns, to convert the rudder into a telemark and, if the wave starts to break, then to convert the telemark into a low paddle brace.

Turning Strokes on the Move

STERN RUDDER One of the most important strokes in canoe surfing, the stern rudder is done while the canoe is travelling forwards by being either paddled or carried on a following sea.

The paddle is placed vertically into the water at the rear of the canoe (Figure 26), the back of the blade facing outwards from the canoe. The blade is then pushed outwards, causing the boat in the illustration to turn to the left. Because there is no support in this stroke, the blade cannot be leant upon, unless the canoe is moving very fast.

Depending on the hull shape, the turn may be easier if the canoe is made to lean on the *opposite* side to the paddle stroke. This will be discovered by practice in your own canoe.

LOW TELEMARK This is a turn to be done at speed. The back of the paddle, which is held in the normal paddle position, is presented to the water. In Figure 27 the right arm is passed in front of the body. The left arm is almost straight with the knuckles turned downwards. The angle of the blade is such that it planes on the surface of the water, enabling the paddler to lean right over onto the blade, getting plenty of support. The canoe in the illustration should turn to its left, but if its hull shape is one that is likely to skid, the man may find himself turning to the right, in

Figure 27. Low telemark turn, canoe moving forwards fast. The paddler leans over and is supported on the back of the blade as it planes on the surface of the water.

which case, with practice, there is no need to change sides. In surf or a following sea this often happens. The man finishes up actually leaning *down* the face of the wave, the paddle stroke on the outside of the turn. To change direction quickly, as on the face of a moving wave, by pushing downwards at the beginning of the stroke, the stern can be lifted and jerked sideways, turning the canoe sharply and enabling it to zigzag on the face of a wave.

ADVANCED TECHNIQUES

Launching in Dumping Surf

In a launching of this kind it is better if the most experienced person goes last. When the others are all ready in their canoes with their spray covers on, he can hold each one steady, time the waves for the lull, then push them out. When his turn comes he holds himself steady on the steeply sloping beach, and as the last surge comes up the beach from the last big 'set' or group of waves, he pushes himself off, using the water as it runs down the slope. He must beware that it does not twist him sideways, beam on to the next approaching wave. If this does happen, it is no time for a heroic paddle brace. He should jump out quickly if he can, get clear of the canoe and leave it. To stay with it may mean an injury.

Landing in Dumping Surf

Study any surf as it rolls in to the beach. There will be six to eight large waves, then usually a pause with much smaller waves. Sometimes the swell may even die out altogether. Then far out to sea the dark ridge parallel to the horizon can be seen as another big set marches majestically shorewards. (See Chapter 5.)

The three men in Figure 28 are all in different stages of negotiating the nasty dumping shore waves on a steeply sloping beach. Number 1 sat watching the waves. Every time one came up behind him he back paddled so as not to be hurled forwards on the face of the wave. When a big set died down he paddled forwards very hard *on the back* of the wave as he is doing in the illustration. This will carry him up the steeply sloping beach. Number 2 got as far up the beach as he could on the surge of water from the broken wave. He stopped himself being sucked back into the next wave by holding himself on his paddle and his hand. Then, *very* quickly, he jumped out, grasped his canoe and paddle and ran up the beach out of the way of the next bone crusher. Number 3 hasn't managed things so well. Although he landed well, he threw his paddle up the beach while the surge was still going up the beach, and then when he was half out of the cockpit the water started to come back down the slope again, taking him with it into the next nasty curling wave.

Figure 28. Landing in dumping surf.

Figure 29. A seal launching.

Seal Launching and Landing

Many of the areas which provide beautiful scenery and freedom for the sea canoeist also provide rocks, cliffs and many difficulties for landings and launchings. Fortunately or unfortunately, seas have a habit of calming down while one is asleep in a tent. Upon walking down to a large flat slab which was regularly awash the day before, you may discover it many feet above a placid sea. The seal launching method in Figure 29 shows a way of getting your canoe safely into the water.

E

Figure 30. Seal landings. In A the canoeist watches and times the swell as it rises up and covers the proposed landing place. The wave must not break too heavily over the rock, nor must there be insufficient water. When the chosen time comes, as the swell swamps the rock, the canoeist paddles hard, having first chosen the smoothest place on which to land. In B once the paddler is directly over the spot where he wishes to land, he must paddle even harder to stop his canoe from being sucked back off the rock by the retreating swell. The moment he feels the canoe touch bottom, he must leap out and quickly drag the boat to safety, thereby avoiding the next wave and clearing the landing place for the next man.

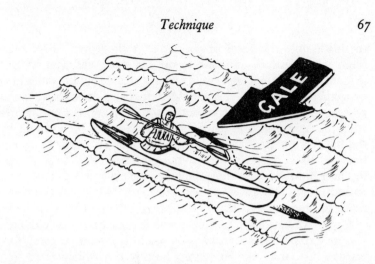

Figure 31. Forward paddling in a beam gale. The man is paddling forwards with a gale force wind blowing on his left side. The waves are close together. As he paddles forwards he will find this much easier if, as the wave hits him, he angles the paddle blade as he sweeps it backwards with his left hand; this means that the stroke on the left side is more of a propulsive paddle brace than a normal forward stroke. The angled blade will thus allow the paddler to lean well over into the wind.

Depending on the room available on the rocks, it might be necessary to launch sideways. With rudders and skegs, which are awkward in this situation, it might be advisable to launch backwards so that the skeg hangs in space and then hits the water first, rather than catching and hooking it on all the rocks while the launch is in progress.

In the seal landing, illustrated in Figure 30, the canoeist follows very closely the procedure for landing in dumping surf.

Wind Techniques

In a beam gale, wriggle down as far as you can in your cockpit; doing this will give the wind less to grab. Lean over onto the wind. Keep the paddle blade on the windward side low. If things get really bad, at the end of the forward stroke, let the back of the blade skim the water on its way back. The wind will tend to push the blade onto the water or cut across it altogether, rather than catch it underneath and tear it up and over, and you with it (Figure 31). A strong gust could take the paddle out of your hands altogether, or else, if you managed to hang on tightly, could capsize you by whipping the paddle over in an arc. If a gust comes from the right, say, and the right-hand blade has been caught by the full force of a violent gust and it is about to take off, do not hold on. Relax the grip with your right hand and let the paddle flip over onto your left side, allowing your left wrist to twist over with the loom. This way you will keep your paddle and you won't finish up underwater.

If you are battling into a head wind, remember that although you may think you are making no headway, you'll be going forwards a little at a time. Hunch up, keep your head down and stop the salt spray lashing at your face and eyes. Try to shut your mind off from the flying spray and the white tops breaking all around you. Get a nice rhythm going and punch your way through, always forwards. Your body can do it; if anything lets you down it will be your will-power.

When crossing the entrace to a bay, remember that any strong offshore wind will produce large waves once the protection of the land is left behind. A safer course, although a much longer one, will therefore be to hug the shore, leaving open crossings for calmer days. A gap in high protective cliffs or hills (Figure 33) can cause any strong winds to accelerate because of a funnelling effect and therefore much stronger gusts can be expected and must be allowed for.

FERRY GLIDE   When any boat is held at an angle to fast-moving water or, in the case of much sea canoeing, at an angle to the wind, it will move sideways across the main flow. In river canoeing, this is called the ferry glide because of its associations with flying ferries on fast-moving rivers. At sea, the manoeuvre is still loosely referred to as the ferry glide, although it would be more technically correct to call it 'making an allowance for set and drift'. This manoeuvre on open water can be a very prolonged affair and using it to travel across several miles is a very different matter from using it to cross a narrow river or even the narrows between two islands (Figure 35).

Figure 32. Turning the kayak in a high wind. In A, the man, leaning into the wind, does a strong reverse sweep with the paddle in the extended position. The strain on the paddle is very great; care must be taken not to break it. In B, the wave passing under the canoe puts the bow clear of the water and gives a moving pivot on which to turn the canoe by a forward sweep stroke using an extended paddle.

Figure 33. Downdraughts. In strong winds, the downblast from a high headland can come as quite a surprise—sudden, violent and usually of a greater velocity than the wind that caused it.

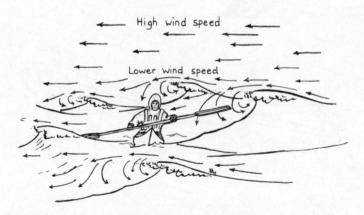

Figure 34. Wind eddies behind waves. The man keeps his arms low while paddling forwards, especially on the windward side. He is sheltered to some extent by the wind eddying behind each wave. Every time he reaches a crest, when his left hand is moving forwards to start the next stroke, he will plane the back of the blade along the crest, thus preventing the wind from snatching at the paddle blade.

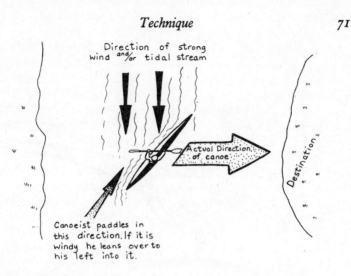

Figure 35. The ferry glide.

This is when the use of transit bearings (see Chapter 8 on navigation) really proves a blessing. A compass is almost useless in this situation, as the canoeist has no means of calculating even the approximate speed of the wind when he is paddling. The only way to ensure a straight ferry glide across the wind is by selecting transit markers.

When the canoeist looks across a channel, the fastest flowing water is always marked by a whitetopped broken wave. If the strong current is opposed by even a moderate wind, it will produce a short, steep chop. This is because the waves are foreshortened or compressed by the wind, causing them to break. So during the crossing of a wide channel, beware when the tide changes against the wind. It could produce conditions that might prove a nightmare, if not a complete disaster, for normal proficiency standard canoeists. In windy weather be sure to make a specific note of what time the tide turns.

The Eskimo Roll

The Eskimo roll is the skill of righting the kayak after it has capsized. It is hardly surprising that the Eskimo invented this

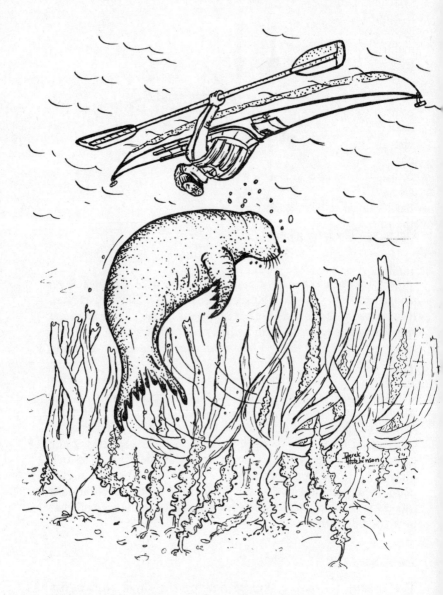

Figure 36. A window into a new world.

system of self-rescue. The water in the Arctic being as cold as it is, any swim may well be the last. During the winter in some areas the Eskimo actually laced his seal-skin anorak tightly onto the manhole rim, making an exit from the canoe impossible and a roll the only way of ensuring survival.

During extreme conditions out in the open sea, a bail-out could prove hazardous, not only for the man in the water, but also for his companions, who might be stretched to the limit themselves in dealing with the situation. Furthermore, any rescue would be virtually impossible in very rough seas or high winds, or inshore near cliffs during a heavy swell or over reefs at sea. A coaching colleague once had the rather horrifying experience of being swept along sideways, upside down in the blackness of a sea cave, and having to roll up with the broken ends of his canoe jammed against the rock sides. In circumstances such as this, any other type of rescue would obviously be almost impossible.

However, a good deal of sea canoeing has been done by a large number of people who cannot, and have no desire to, roll a canoe. But having the ability increases confidence and improves your whole attitude towards the sea and rough water canoeing.

There are also much happier uses for a good rolling technique. It is necessary for any high degree of competence in surf work. And when you are armed with a face mask on a warm summer's day, it gives you a window into a world which is denied to everyone else except divers.

The best way to learn to roll is to get a properly qualified instructor to teach you personally. Go to a baths course organised by a British Canoe Union coach. The water will be nice and warm, and there is the comfort of having someone standing next to you while you are under water. Wearing a face mask or a nose clip makes the experience even less unpleasant by making possible a clear view while upside down, and preventing water shooting up the nose.

There are a series of confidence exercises which can be done in the pool before the roll proper is even touched upon. For instance, it is good training to hold onto the pipe at the bath side and practise turning upside down and pulling yourself up to the surface again, thus getting the correct 'hip flick'. Capsizing the canoe and swimming to the side of the pool without getting out of the canoe is another exercise in confidence. It is possible to push up and get a gulp of air while you are swimming if need be.

Before starting to roll make sure you and the kayak are as one. A tight, snug-fitting moulded seat, thigh grips, knee supports or bars, and if possible a fitted footrest, are needed to make sure you wear the canoe, rather than just sit in it loosely.

For sea canoeing it is not necessary to be able to roll both sides. If, for instance, you capsize on your good side, do a normal roll. If you capsize on your wrong side in a broken wave, the wave will force you round and bring you up into the paddle brace or support position. If you capsize in turbulence, hang upside down until the turbulence stops and then roll up in the normal way.

The roll which my associates used to teach first at one time was the 'Put across roll'. The paddle was pushed out from the side and at one stage it was not under full control because the hand grip was rather loose, so that if the water was at all lively the paddle tended to be swept away. This particular roll, therefore, does not merit inclusion in a sea canoeing book because of this possible danger.

PAWLATA ROLL   In my opinion the Pawlata (Figure 37) is the best roll to teach a beginner. Many of my coaching colleagues would support this view because the screw roll, the most important roll of all, is a direct progression from the Pawlata. But so long as you can roll first time every time, then the particular technique used is irrelevant.

If you have difficulty with the Pawlata, think about the following points:

1. The *angle* of the blade as it moves from the canoe must be such that it planes out and along the *surface*.
2. You must lean forwards.
3. The roll should be executed with great vigour.
4. Don't try to roll before you are upside down.
5. The forwards arm is swept out to the side in an arc by the *straight arm, not* pulled downwards.
6. Don't forget to push the left arm *forwards* and to the surface; otherwise the blade will hit the side of the canoe, and you will not be able to sweep the forward blades outwards.
7. After the sweep outwards with the right hand, the upper part of the right arm should *brush past the nose* and *over the head* as you break the surface. Failing to do this is the most common reason for failure.

SCREW ROLL   This is probably the most important roll of all, because the basic position of the hands on the paddle loom remains unaltered. Sometimes the paddler becomes unsure of his hand position in relation to the angle of the paddle blades. This is no problem with looms which are slightly oval in the area of the hand position. Aluminium looms can be shaped by squeezing them in a vice. If in doubt, the paddler can move the nearest hand quickly along the loom until it reassuringly touches the blade in a recognisable position and then put it back in place for the commencement of the roll. With practice, it will not be necessary to move the hands from the normal paddling position. Because the leverage is shorter, a higher degree of skill is required for this than for any other roll.

It is during the performance of this roll that we discover another advantage of using the longer, narrower sea paddle. The roll is made easier because the upper blade does not have to be pushed up as high to clear the bottom of the canoe. The blade which, in the meantime, is sweeping outwards on the surface of the water is also at a better angle for the downwards stroke of the roll proper.

KING ISLAND ROLL   An Alaskan roll of King Island is shown in Figure 38. This is done with a single paddle blade. It will be seen that when the paddler is in the inverted position, the paddle is held at arm's length downwards. During the sweep round, the blade, because of its angle, takes a rising path towards the surface and finishes up in a position behind the man. The remaining forward sweep, bringing the man upright, reminds one of the European Steyr roll shown in Figure 39.

While hunting in the rough waters of the Bering Sea, a man could be caught by a sudden capsize. If unable to roll up with his paddle, he could withdraw himself up into the roomy body of his kayak and wait until his comrade paddled to his assistance and turned him upright again. It has not been unknown for a hunter who has lost his paddle to attempt a roll using his throwing-stick, and sometimes in desperation even attempting to use the blade of his knife.

Other rolls include the Eskimo storm roll (Figure 40), the vertical storm roll (Figure 41) and the Greenland roll (Figure 42). The ultimate in kayak rolling is the no-paddle roll, otherwise known as the hand roll.

Text continued on page 83.

Figure 37. The Pawlata roll.

So you want to roll. Well are you sitting comfortably? Good. The paddle is on your left side. Hold the nearest blade at the top corner, thumb downwards, fingers inside. Don't reach too far forwards with the right hand; the knuckles should be uppermost looking away from the canoe. The outward edge of the forward paddle blade can be tilted slightly towards the water. Are you ready? Right, take a deep breath and capsize. Turn the page round now, and keep holding your breath!

Wait, open your eyes, study the picture. Try to orientate yourself— good. Don't panic; it's only water. Bend your body and push your face towards the surface. Push your hands upwards towards the surface. Swing out with your right-hand blade, the outward edge tilted upwards as it planes out in an arc along the surface. Keep that right arm almost straight. The left hand pushes up out of the water and forwards.

You should be in the position indicated in (A) as your head breaks the surface. Your right bicep should have just pushed past your nose. Push down hard—you have just completed your first Pawlata roll.

A

Figure 38. King Island roll.

The paddler sits in the middle of the large manhole with his back unsupported. He hooks his knees under the first thwart forward of the cockpit. This roll is a good one for a tired paddler; it is a gradual roll, spreading the righting action over a longer period.

The paddle is held out in front of the body horizontally. The paddle blade sticks out to the left. The kayaker is now in the position for the capsize.

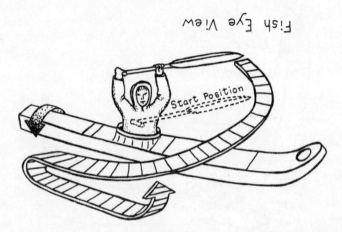

The arms can be extended during the capsize or immediately afterwards. To roll up, the paddle is swept forward as indicated; the leading edge of the blade planes towards the surface during its sweep round. This must be done with some speed to gain lift towards the surface. The change of direction for the forward sweep must also be executed quickly, so as not to lose the momentum of the rising sweep round. This roll can be done successfully with a double-bladed paddle.

Figure 39. Steyr roll.

Hold the paddle as if for the Pawlata. Then lie back along the rear deck, with the right arm either above the head as in (A) or across the face as in (B). This is a most uncomfortable position, especially for the left hand. You will also feel unstable. Twist the top half of your body to the left, then capsize on that side.

Wait until you are hanging upside down and your head is twisted back looking at the rear of the canoe. Push the right hand and arm across your face and out to the side. Push down as the paddle sweeps out, and you will rise to the surface.

Much less effort is needed for this than for other rolls, but it lacks popularity because the preparatory position or 'wind up' is a difficult one to adopt under water.

Figure 40. Eskimo storm roll.

This is a true Eskimo roll as used by the Eskimos of the Angmassalik area of Greenland. The starting position or 'wind up' is rather like the Pawlata, except that the forward paddle blade is at an angle of 30° from the side of the canoe.

Lean well forward and push upwards with the right hand, so that the forward paddle blade is about a foot above the surface. Now pull down violently. You will rise very quickly. The paddle goes down vertically for about one foot, then starts to plane outwards as the roll nears completion.

Figure 41. Vertical storm roll.

Use the same wind-up position as the Storm Roll.

Fish Eye View

The blade when pushed above the surface is in a vertical position. The edge of the blade nearest the water is angled slightly outwards from the canoe, so that although the blade bites down very deeply—2 to 3 ft., it will eventually slice outwards and down for maximum support.

Figure 42. Greenland roll.

It has been thought, quite wrongly, that because a kayak is very unstable when the right way up, it is easy to roll when upside down. It is obvious that the bottom hull shape, apart from its narrowness, exerts very little influence on the kayak when it is being rolled. However if the deck has a 'banana' shape lengthwise, when the boat is upside down it will try to turn on its side, upon which it will normally readily float. This action is assisted by the buoyancy of the canoeist's body. Boat and man finish up at an angle of about 45° to the surface of the water (B), the kayak in many cases showing an almost flat bottom to the sky. In this position the man is ready to start the roll.

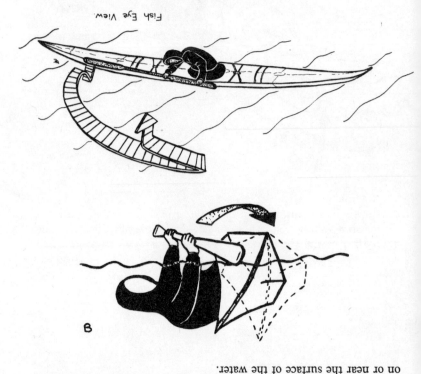

The paddle is held alongside the canoe with the blade in a vertical position. The blade angle is altered as it leaves the side of the kayak. It is then planed outwards. This can bring the man to the surface, or the roll may be finished off by a quick forwards scull, the paddle blade finishing on or near the surface of the water.

HAND ROLL

1. An assistant is needed at first. He stands on your right-hand side.
2. Lean well back in the cockpit to touch the back of your head on the rear deck.
3. Place the knuckles of your right hand well behind your left ear, palm outwards.
4. Capsize on your left side. Keep your head touching the back deck.
5. Your partner will put his upwards facing palm in a position where it touches your downwards facing palm. Hook your fingers into his.
6. Sweep your arm violently in a wide sweeping arc towards the bottom of the bath and follow through until your right arm is fully extended sideways.
7. As you break the surface, fling the left arm forcibly over sideways; this will assist the momentum.

This exercise will give you confidence. Next try the same with a table tennis bat or a polystyrene float. You can assist the first part of the roll by dog-paddling to the surface first on the right-hand side. Now quickly, head on the back deck, fling your right arm downwards and round with great force, throwing your left hand out as a counterbalance, to help the last part of the roll.

Once you have learnt to roll, practise at every opportunity, especially in rough conditions; surf is ideal because a failure means only a short swim.

Always keep calm when you are upside down. Worry makes your heart beat faster. This takes more oxygen, which is un-obtainable. So keep cool and think about something else. You will be surprised just how long you can happily hold your breath: you should be able to do so for about 30 seconds, if not a little longer. The time will depend on many factors—some physical, some psychological, some environmental (the temperature of the water is a factor).

Some people have taught that one's time under water can be lengthened by *hyperventilation*. 'Overbreathing increases the endurance time by removing carbon dioxide from the body and delaying the time at which its concentration builds up again to the point at which it produces an irresistible stimulus to breathe. The overbreathing does not appreciably increase the amount of oxygen stored in the body, as the haemoglobin of arterial blood is almost saturated with oxygen even during normal breathing.'[*] If you exclude carbon dioxide from your body for too long, you will lose the desire to breathe, and after doing the longest underwater-hang on record, you will quite painlessly lose consciousness and subsequently drown. In all rolling practice it is vital to have qualified instructors near at hand in case anyone unwittingly induces hyperventilation.

*W. R. Keatinge, *Survival in Cold Water*, Blackwell Scientific Publishers, 1969, p. 99.

3
Surfing

Equipment

The power of surf is tremendous. In big waves I have seen a number of canoes snap in half with the occupants still sitting in them and once I even saw a canoe 'pop out' of the water quite empty, while the man, complete with spray cover attached to the cockpit rim and seat, struggled to swim ashore still in his ejection seat! Buy the best and strongest equipment you can.

CANOES Any canoe will surf. But if the keel is straight, manoeuvring on the waves is out of the question. A well-rockered glass-fibre slalom canoe is the type most widely used, reinforced with either extra layers of glassfibre, Diolen or carbon-fibre strips which can be incorporated in the 'lay up' during manufacture. Another type is the specialised surf canoe described at the end of this chapter.

My slalom canoe weighs about 45 lb. but even 10 lb. less than this would still be fine. Added strength comes from the canoe's buoyancy. Air bags tailored to the canoe's shape or large dinghy bags can be blown up in position, preventing any flexing of the hull and deck. Polystyrene blocks touching the top of the deck and bottom of the hull can also be used to give support although they are not sufficient on their own. Every available spare inch of the canoe's interior should be filled with some sort of flotation material that cannot leave the canoe in the event of a capsize.

SPRAY COVERS More advanced surfers have usually worn two

85

spray covers of the nylon neoprene or nylon PVC type. Spray
covers of neoprene wet-suit material lined with nylon are becoming more and more popular, as they are extremely watertight
and flex with the movements of the canoeist's body. All spray
covers should have a quick-release strap or toggle, especially the
rubber wet-suit material type, which can be fitted tighter than
those made of less stretchy material. Spray covers should be tight,
but when they have to come off, they must come off quickly.

The funnel or sleeve which fits around the body should be
higher on a surfing spray cover than on those used for normal
canoeing. This is so that it can be worn tucked up under the lifejacket waist strap, thus preventing the apron being forced downwards by the weight of the water pressing upon it. Some spray
covers are fitted with shoulder straps to stop this.

LIFEJACKETS AND BUOYANCY AIDS Any spectator at a canoe
surfing championship will notice that most of the competitors
wear buoyancy aids rather than lifejackets. The competitors
justify this on several grounds. As noted in the preceding chapter,
a lifejacket must be inflated in order to float the wearer face upwards and provide maximum buoyancy. However, it should not
be worn inflated, and when deflated, it provides less buoyancy
than one of the better buoyancy aids. Bearing in mind that surfing
accidents happen suddenly and that they frequently involve lung
or head injuries resulting in loss of consciousness, one must ask
who supplies the air to blow up the lifejacket and convert it from
an inefficient buoyancy aid to a life-saving device. On the other
hand, buoyancy aids provide reasonably effective body armour and
seem to give greater freedom around the neck. A lifejacket has to
be tied tight around the body, and since surfing is often done without the buffering effect of a wet-suit jacket, the straps can cut
uncomfortably into the canoeist's sides and back. The added
buoyancy of wet-suit trousers also seems to inhibit the true lifejacket from doing its job properly. Capsizes in surf do not always
result in injury but frequently make necessary very long swims
to shore, with or without a canoe, and such swims are much easier
with a buoyancy aid than with a lifejacket.

Whatever you decide to use, make sure *you wear it*, tied, buckled
or zipped up securely. To surf wearing no personal buoyancy at all

is absolute madness and can endanger not only your life but the lives of those who will have to rescue you.

CRASH HELMETS These are a must. It is not so much that one's head bounces more easily off the sea bottom, but rather that it bounces more safely off other people's canoes, with or without occupants, and airborne surfboards without riders. Bailing out on the inshore side of your own canoe when a wave is about to break can cause a head injury without a crash helmet.

The best types are those which come well down over the ears, low over the forehead and well down at the back. I have two helmets, a climbing helmet in which I drilled holes and a Romer crash hat, both of which are very good. Some helmets which were originally designed for ice hockey don't really give enough protection around the ears, while others, although they have a well-designed bowl, are tilted backwards by a badly positioned chin strap which tends to press against the Adam's apple and cause great discomfort if worn in the correct position.

TOGGLES For hanging onto the canoe in the water, toggles at the bow and stern are essential. Rope loops tend to twist round and trap the fingers if the canoe starts to twist in the water.

FOOTREST My footrest is a piece of very strong oval gymnasium wallbar glassed solidly into position. It cannot be altered, of course, but if you are not lending anyone the boat or selling it this is probably ideal since nothing on earth will move or snap it. Some go-ahead manufacturers fit fail-safe footrests so that if by some misfortune feet are forced past and behind it, they can be withdrawn by swinging the footrest out and around as they do so.

Any system that will not allow your feet to slip past or that will not break when the sudden weight of the body hits it during a pole vault off the bottom will do fine. But remember that bolts can sheer through, and if the deck and hull of the boat compress, the sides will move outwards, springing the footrest free and causing you to fall past into the front of the canoe.

Techniques

Surfing—the ability to handle violently breaking waves, to run with them, battle out against them and take them on the beam—is probably the best training anyone can have for tackling rough water out at sea. However, surfing is not sea canoeing. There are many men and women who love the sea and canoe on it to a very high standard but who prefer not to enter the world of surf acrobatics, just as surely as there are some virtuosos in surf acrobatics who wouldn't dream of rolling a canoe way out at sea, and who certainly haven't got the stamina or mature outlook for prolonged sea expedition work in rough water. Doubly happy are they who can both surf and sea canoe.

Canoe surfing, which can soon draw a crowd, appeals to the exhibitionist in all of us. It is also rather like a drug: every loop is going to be the last before lunch, and the last . . . and the last, till the aching, happy, hungry canoeists drag themselves from the water like so many worn-out selchies.*

Surf is the white water of the sea. It is exhilarating and exciting but it can be dangerous if not treated with respect. Surfing utilises the basic sea canoeing skills—the stern rudder, low telemark and paddle brace. With just these basic skills, quite a high standard of skill can be yours, although for big surf and acrobatics, an ability to roll is essential.

To embark on your surfing career, first choose a companion— you *never* surf alone—and choose a day when the waves are not too large. Start by sitting in the 'soup'; this is the broken wave as it tumbles to shore. Let yourself become used to the feeling of paddling about and paddle bracing if need be.

FORWARD RUNNING Paddle out a few yards, turn and point your bow shorewards. When a small broken wave is a few feet behind you, paddle forwards. The wave will catch you up, and you will feel yourself seemingly hurtle forwards. Try to keep your balance and steer with a stern rudder. The canoe is bound to turn either left or right, so let your rudder convert into a low brace and lean on it, not too much, just enough for support, and you'll move sideways, upright, having just surfed your first small wave. Keep practising, and when you feel confident, go out to the green waves beyond the break. Wait until a fairly steep humping wave is about 5 or 6 yd. behind you; then paddle forwards fast, leaning

*A mythical sea creature—half man, half seal—of the Scottish outer islands.

forwards. As the wave catches up, your stern will be lifted, and you will be carried in more or less planing on the face of the wave, depending on its angle and speed. Steady and control your run with a stern rudder. You might have to change sides quickly to keep running straight. Eventually the canoe will swing to either one side or the other. If it keeps running straight you must choose a side on which to turn. Then as the wave towers steeply over you and you are parallel to it, either do a vigorous stern rudder, which will take you back over the top of the wave just before it starts to break, or, if it starts to break and you are still on its face as your paddle is trailing down, flip over into the paddle brace position and hang on as your paddle is supported on the upsurge inside the wave as it breaks and sweeps you to the beach.

If you see someone paddling out and you think you are on an eventual collision course with him, capsize. The weight of your body upside down will stop the forward momentum of the canoe. Then if you can roll up, do so. If not, bail out and tow your boat and paddle to shore, pulling it in by a lively back stroke. If a large

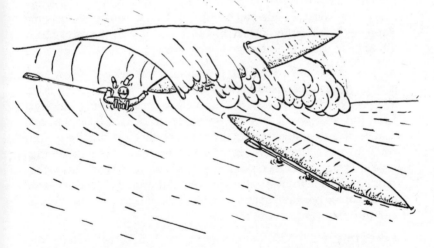

Figure 43. A typical surfing situation. Note the man rolling to protect himself while the capsized man hangs on to his paddle as well as his canoe.

wave looms up, don't look along your upturned hull at it; otherwise when it picks up your boat and stands it on end, it will harpoon you. Instead move to one side slightly, hold on tight and let the canoe be thrown shorewards (Figure 43). You'll be glad you're holding a toggle and not a loop as the canoe twists round and round.

A word of warning! Do not capsize if you are on top of a breaking wave and someone is paddling out immediately to one side of you and inshore. You will be skewered upside down on his bow. Sit tight and paddle brace. He must capsize and allow you to pass over his upturned hull. He will then either roll up or bail out, depending on his skill.

During the slow tow to the beach, keep the canoe upside down, even if it is full of buoyancy; otherwise breaking waves will fill what space there is, and the surge will then float your aquarium up onto the sand, there to stand immovable because of the weight of water, slowly splitting and cracking at the seams. If your swamped canoe is in danger of being beached the right way up, quickly drag it back into about 2 ft. of water and either turn it upside down so that at least it will drain itself out when beached—it tends to get full of sand this way—or get someone to help you empty it in thigh-deep water. While you do this, don't get parallel to inshore 'soup', as it will either knock the canoe out of your hands or keep filling it up again as fast as you empty it.

REVERSE RUNNING Face the green oncoming waves. When one is a few yards away, lean backwards and start back-paddling fast. The canoe will be picked up and will move backwards quickly. Lean forwards up the wave as the angle steepens. The canoe will change direction quicker than it does when forward running, so be ready to place the paddle in near the bow and do a ruddering stroke. If, say, the canoe swings violently to your right, allow the ruddering blade to trail and swing out and over the wave into the paddle brace position, supporting you as you lean onto the paddle and into the wave.

PADDLING OUT THROUGH LARGE SURF It is best to paddle out fast in the lull between sets, helped if possible by a rip current from the beach. Watch out you don't mistime things; otherwise you could find yourself a hundred yards out from the shore with a huge set bearing down upon you. If this happens you must employ techniques such as the following.

Paddle fast towards the oncoming wave. As it looms up in front of you, if you think you can lean back without the canoe being hurled backwards into an unwelcome reverse loop, do so; the shock of its hitting you will be lessened. Otherwise lean well forwards, keep paddling and punch your way through and watch the wave doesn't remove your crash helmet. The difficulty is trying to judge whether it is possible to slacken off your forward paddling to minimise the impact with the wave, or whether this would again send you backwards. Doing this I once had my own paddle loom smashed against my forehead—before crash hats were as popular as they are now—producing a lump the size of an egg above one eye.

Perhaps the best way of coping with the whole situation is to roll over as the wave is a few yards away so that when it strikes, you will be hanging, nice and safe, upside down. The canoe will perhaps move about quite vigorously and you will get that washing machine feeling around the head. When all goes still again, roll up quickly. Keep paddling out fast, and hope you can beat the next wave before it breaks.

Before you start your run, look behind on the side to which you are likely to turn and make sure that no one is in your way. Remember where everyone is and in what direction they are paddling in relation to your proposed run. Then look behind on the other side in case the wave alters your plans.

TRACKING OR CUTTING BACK If the wave is a very large one, the canoe will run down the face into the trough in front of it. It will lose speed dramatically as the planing speed is lost. The breaking wave will then overtake you in a welter of spray and foam, leaving you to paddle brace and mourn the loss of a superb wave which farther along its length has not even broken yet.

To avoid this, as you surf in, look along the wave in both directions quickly and determine on which side the wave will start to break. Do a sharp stern rudder on the opposite side to the curling wave. The canoe will then travel almost parallel to the sloping wave. Not only will the canoe be moving sideways but it will also be climbing towards the crest again. Then lean down the wave slope into a low telemark, converting into a stern rudder as the canoe once again faces down the wave, but this time much higher up its face. Keep cutting back like this, using all the wave has to offer. If you wish to leave the wave, track close the to crest; a sharp stern rudder jerked outwards on the side of the crest will cause the canoe to flip over the back of the wave.

Although you had a clear run to the beach when you started, you may now have moved 80 to 100 yd. sideways into an overpopulated area full of bathers. Don't allow your canoe to hurtle sideways as the wave breaks, scything a path 15 ft. wide through small children and nervous swimmers. Either pull off the wave in the normal manner or capsize and hope that the weight of your body will slow you down. Once you are paddle bracing on a large wave, all the capsizing in the world won't stop you if you are parallel. Only by capsizing at a slight angle to the break will you have any chance of slowing down.

Surf Acrobatics

THE LOOP If you surf long enough, the day is bound to arrive when, quite accidentally, the nose of your canoe digs in and suddenly, before you realise it, the whole thing goes end over end, and you have just done your first loop. At the end of the day you'll tell your admiring friends all about it and how easy it was.

What makes the canoe do this ? Well, when a wave is critical, it is in a state where its steepness does not allow a normal slalom canoe to plane in a controlled manner down its slope. Instead it will plunge down to the bottom of the wave, burying its bow deep. You will not have to paddle forwards to make it do this. Thus at an angle of about 60° all forward movement is arrested at the bow while the moving wave still pushes the rest of the canoe into an upright position called the loop position. The bow of the canoe may touch the bottom—a pole vault—or it may stand on end and use its own buoyancy for support. The rest of the canoe then falls over, completing the loop. Although it all looks quite horrific to the uninitiated, it is the stern of the canoe which performs the large arc through the air, *not your body*. Your head travels perhaps only in an arc of 3 or 4 ft. while the loop is in progress, because when the canoe stands on its end the wave carries on, giving you a soft bed to fall upon. Thus you will not finish your loop way down

Figure 44. The loop. Lean well forwards and wind up into a roll position. You will be over and up before you know what has happened.

below in the distant trough, but on the *back* of the wave. If you lean forwards, as you will if you prepare yourself for a roll, your head will hardly travel any distance at all (Figure 44).

A loop can be done as a finale to a run when the wave is about to break, or else the canoeist can wait at the break line catching the waves when they are too steep for a run, allowing the bow to plunge into a loop.

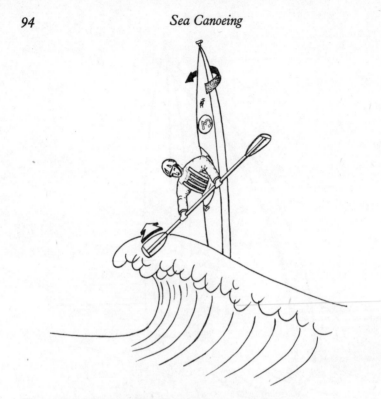

Figure 45. Loop and flick (or simple pirouette).

FLICK AND PIROUETTE   The upright loop position can also be
the start of other exciting manoeuvres. By reaching down with
the paddle blade into the water, a quick push and hip flick will
turn the canoe so that as it falls back down, it will be facing out to
sea again and you won't even get wet (Figure 45). This is a spec-
tacular trick but it can be improved upon.

   With the canoe upright standing on its bow, you can stand on
the footrest, your body at right angles, paddle held slightly to the
left side. Straighten the body quickly, your head travelling in the
direction of the back deck. As you do so, fling round both arms,
holding the paddle across to the right, violently twisting around to
the right from the thighs. With practice the canoe will spin round
and round in a pirouette.

This is an extremely difficult trick, requiring a lot of practice. A friend of mine in Bristol, a winner of many surfing prizes, can do this without a paddle, having dispensed with it at the beginning of his run down the wave. If necessary, he can do the loop, pirouette and roll, all without a paddle.

REVERSE LOOP   This is the forward loop in reverse, quite simple and requiring perhaps less courage than the forward loop because your body tends to be nearer the water during the actual loop and it is your back which is presented to the water, not your face and front.

Figure 46. Eskimo loop or Reverse loop and flick.

Figure 47. Pop-out.

Watch out for a reverse pole vault. This can cause you to jerk backwards, leaving the footrest and jarring the spine against the coaming. A back strap is handy there, alhough I prefer to have inflated buoyancy protruding into the rear of the cockpit and then jambing a polystyrene bath float between it and the seat to absorb any shock.

ESKIMO LOOP OR REVERSE LOOP AND FLICK This is probably the most graceful trick in surf acrobatics (Figure 46). As the canoe is running backwards down the wave, the stern will begin to dig in. Just before it reaches the vertical position, the canoeist winds up into the screw roll position. He then rolls into the wave, rotating the canoe vertically on its point through 180°. As the front end of

John Thorburn

1. Seal launchings can be made easier at low tide by the thick carpet of seaweed. The boat is held back on it until the paddler is ready to let himself slide into the water.

2. The Gulf of Corryvreckan between Jura and Scarba. The Great Whirlpool—'The Hag'—can be clearly seen, near the centre, with its accompanying tide race and overfall. The main flood stream is moving from left to right, but the water at the bottom of the picture is moving from right to left. The distance from coast to coast is one sea mile.

P. & H. Fibreglass

3. A surfing action shot of two 'Surfer' canoes.

4. Sue Chappell of the Corps of Canoe Life Guards returning to shore with a patient—stern carry.

Youth Activities Centre, Weymouth

British Industrial Plastics

5. The slender thread between sea and inland canoeing. This is river canoeing, but the wave is caused by a tidal bore, approximately 2 ft. 6 in. high. The men are using 'Surf-Shoe' canoes; in the foreground, Frank Goodman is per-forming a stern rudder on his right side.

Chris Jowsey

6. A North Sea Kayak, showing equipment secured on the rear deck.

7. Dumping surf can be dangerous, even at the Canoe Surfing Championships, South Shields, 1972.

Derek Holmes

8. Reverse running on a small wave. Note the paddle blade gaining support over and behind the wave, allowing the canoe to run backwards.

9. The author performing a loop and flick at the Canoe Surfing Championships, South Shields, 1972.

Derek Holmes

Paul Quinn

10. The author befriending a young seal on Crumstone, one of the Farne Islands. Such meetings are fairly frequent off the northern coasts of the British Isles.

11. Tom Caskey, BCU coach, in his 'Baidarka', negotiating a narrow passage off the west coast of Scotland.

Alan Harbottle

Bob & Ira Spring

12. Dominic Thomas demonstrating the King Island kayak for tourists in Nome, Alaska.

the canoe continues in its arc through the air, the canoeist will be completing his roll and, hopefully, will find himself continuing his run on the same wave, this time forwards.

POP OUT This is sometimes called a sky-rocket (Figure 47). With practice it is possible to manoeuvre the canoe to the crest of a large wave. The boat will drop down the steep face and, with great force, will bury itself and you down inside the wave. Like a ping-pong ball in a bucket of water the canoe is forced skywards, with any luck completely out of the water. While in this airborne condition you can execute a flick or pirouette, shout in exuberance or perhaps just admire the wonderful view.

Surf Canoes

At first glance, the shape of the early surf canoes belied their performance. Generally fairly narrow with rather squared-off ends, they resembled ungainly surfboards which had grown a top shell. Recent surf canoes have shown a more graceful line, and in the almost flat hull, the tapered flat stern, the upswept front or kick-up and pronounced rail (bottom side edge), they closely resemble Malibu surfboards, whose manoeuvres they can so nearly emulate. As a particular type of craft, surf canoes, regardless of shape or size, can all make manoeuvres in surf which cannot be achieved in other kayaks, sea or slalom.

Perhaps the biggest difference between the surf canoe and the slalom canoe is the ability of the surf canoe, in very large, intimidating surf, to provide one with an escape route. Many times in my slalom canoe, low down on the face of really big waves, with no hope of climbing to the crest and off, I have often wished for some magic way out, perhaps an ejector seat, rather than having to face the alternative of a shoulder-tearing, lung-bursting paddle brace or a particularly violent, uncontrolled somersault. The surf canoe provides this magic way out with its extreme manoeuvrability both on the face of the wave and in the 'soup'.

The surf canoe requires a steep take-off slope, so to start the run the wave should be getting near to its critical pitch. This is because the surf canoe cannot be paddled fast to catch the more gently sloping green waves. You might think that starting on a

G

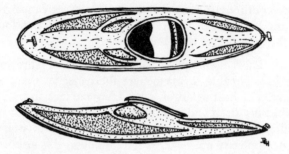

Figure 48. Typical features of a surf canoe. Lengths and widths seem to vary between 7 to 9 ft. and 22 to 24 in. Note the hard rail, sharp kick-up and flat bottom.

steep slope is putting you in a loop position, but the surf canoe rarely loops forwards. Once away, it has the speed to cut across to where the wave is at a less acute angle.

If you are caught in the paddle brace position, don't wonder why the boat will not lean over into the wave. It won't lean: it has a flat bottom. Place the paddle out into the usual position, try to transfer some of your weight onto it and you will probably find that the boat is still upright as the wave breaks. Then with a little practice, instead of paddle bracing all the way to shore, you can lift your paddle above your head in bravado, as the flat bottom of the surf canoe planes and gives you all the support you need.

The surf canoe can run forwards in front of the piled-up 'soup' of huge waves, a feat impossible in a slalom canoe. Its responsive shape makes it easy to cut back and away from that vulnerable position at the base of a wave and makes possible other sudden changes of direction. Its great speed is such that when tracking it can be made to zigzag up and down the wave by rapidly changing from a stern rudder on one side to one on the other, a movement known as a roller coaster. Although it is exciting to perform a roller coaster, travelling at speed along the wave with the breaking curl following behind, the cut back proper is even more exciting. This is cutting back the opposite way, under the breaking curl. The canoe is swiftly and deliberately swung round onto the steepest, most critical part of the wave, to pick up even more speed, before being swung back round again for another roller coaster. This, to me, has always seemed the nearest thing to flying that canoe surfing can offer.

The shape and size of the surf canoe make it possible for a skilled handler to perform 360° spins on the face of a wave while still progressing down the wave—an experience which some find even more exhilarating than the cut back. A number of consecutive spins can be performed on the same wave. For a spin, the surf canoe must be travelling at its fastest, usually when dropping down the face of the wave just after the cut back or during the drop of a roller coaster. As the hull skims and planes down the wave, the canoeist must do a violent reverse sweep with his paddle, moving rapidly from a stern rudder position while pushing hard with the appropriate foot on the footrest to give more power to the paddle stroke. The canoeist must not lean the canoe, but must sit upright, thus keeping the hull flat on the

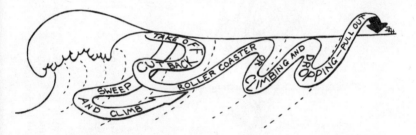

Figure 49. Surf canoe manoeuvres.

Take off when the wave is steep and the crest is at breaking point. Two strokes and the surf canoe will be planing down the wave.

Set your boat at the desired angle by a stern rudder.

When the surf canoe is moving faster than the breaking shoulder, it is possible to *cut back* by dropping down the wave and then turning at a sharp angle back in towards the shoulder.

Another quick turn and the run can continue. By turning the body and stern ruddering, *climbing* and *dropping* is possible, making the surf canoe rise and fall on the face of the wave just ahead of the moving shoulder.

The *sweep* and *climb* is possible only on large slow waves. The boat drops down the wave, is turned into the trough in front of the breaking wave, is quickly spun round 180° and then climbs back up towards the shoulder, escaping the 'soup' and continuing with the run.

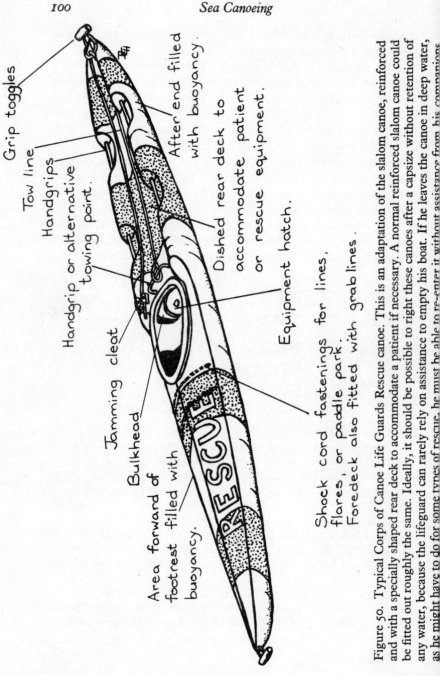

Grip toggles

Tow line

Handgrips

Handgrip or alternative towing point.

Jamming cleat

Bulkhead

Area forward of footrest filled with buoyancy.

After end filled with buoyancy.

Dished rear deck to accommodate patient or rescue equipment.

Equipment hatch.

Shock cord fastenings for lines, flares, or paddle park. Foredeck also fitted with grab lines.

Figure 50. Typical Corps of Canoe Life Guards Rescue canoe. This is an adaptation of the slalom canoe, reinforced and with a specially shaped rear deck to accommodate a patient if necessary. A normal reinforced slalom canoe could be fitted out roughly the same. Ideally, it should be possible to right these canoes after a capsize without retention of any water, because the lifeguard can rarely rely on assistance to empty his boat. If he leaves the canoe in deep water, as he might have to do for some types of rescue, he must be able to re-enter it without assistance from his companions.

sloping face of the wave. Even when broadside onto the wave, the canoe will still be sliding downwards while it is spinning.

The surf canoe must be travelling fast before trying the 360° spin. If by chance the canoe has descended to the lower part of the wave and lost some of its momentum, it will do only a half spin (180°), leaving you looking up the face of a breaking wave while still moving backwards. In this position just resign yourself to a graceful reverse loop. Surf canoes don't do this violently but seem to stand on their tails for a considerable time before flipping over.

People evolve their own combinations of manoeuvres that they enjoy performing. My own favourite is a spin, then a roller coaster followed by a cut back, and then a drop down into another spin until I run out of wave.

Canoe Life Guards

With his knowledge of surf techniques and skills, the canoeist offers a relatively fast method of reaching anyone in distress in open water. He can travel much faster than a swimmer and arrive far less exhausted. The use of a canoe also enables any lifeguard to patrol beyond the surf line or within it if necessary. In this way he can be a welcome addition to any existing rescue facilities, such as inshore rescue boats and rocket lines, and he augments the reel and line team while in no way replacing it.

The Corps of Canoe Life Guards was originally founded to operate in times of flood and natural disaster. Now, however, with its associated Canoe Beach Rescue Units of the Royal Life Saving Society, it has moved away from its original concept and sets a high standard in the field of beach and estuary rescue, life-saving and patrolling techniques.

One of the main purposes of the Corps is to train young people in canoe handling skills so that they in turn will be able to go to the assistance of anyone in, on or under the water. The training is rigorous, as the risks involved are not inconsiderable. It covers a wide and varied programme and is constantly changing as a result of experience, changing conditions, new equipment and more advanced techniques. All lifeguards are trained in the following:

1. A high standard of canoeing ability, i.e. BCU proficiency tests and Coaching awards.

2. Royal Life Saving Society and Surf Life Saving Association methods and awards.
3. First Aid.
4. Signalling.
5. Canoe Life Guards methods of rescue using a combination of canoeing and life-saving techniques varying from unit to unit depending upon local conditions.
6. Patrolling methods, which also vary from unit to unit depending on local conditions.

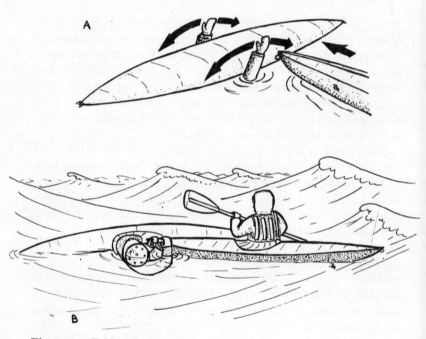

Figure 51. Eskimo bow rescue.
A. Position of hands prior to contact.
B. 'The lift'.

4

Rescues

Capsizing is part of the sport of canoeing. It is what happens after the capsize that is most important. The Eskimo roll is the first line of defence. Of course, rolls can go wrong, paddles can break, strange and weird things can happen to technique on cold windy days when the hands are numb. So the next line of defence is the Eskimo rescue. There comes a time, however, at advanced canoeing standard, in steep breaking seas following close on top of each other, that Eskimo rescues, if indeed possible, should be attempted only with the greatest caution for fear of injury to arms, head and boat.

All rescues, needless to say, must be practised first, preferably in a swimming bath.

Eskimo Bow Rescue

The bow rescue by the Eskimo method is the easier to teach as well as to do and hence is the more common.

When you capsize, quickly bang hard on the bottom of your canoe to attract attention—it really does! Then slowly move the hands fore and aft in an arc (Figure 51A), covering about a yard during the sweep. This gives you more chance of contacting the bow of the canoe which is presented to you, saving your rescuer unnecessary manoeuvring, and of course time. You may feel toggles or the round ending of some Eskimo kayaks. They are very comforting to grasp and give you something to hold on to. Then pull yourself up, as in Figure 51B. In the rescue illustrated the

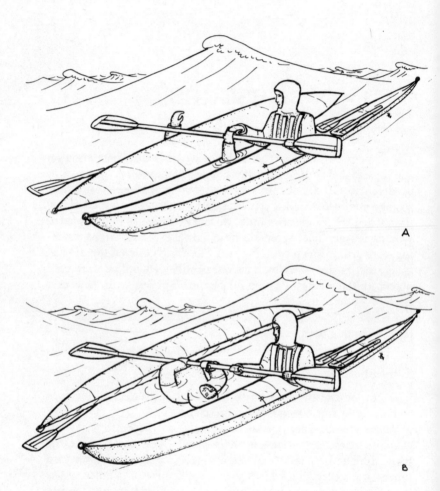

Figure 52. Eskimo side rescue.
A. Guiding the hand.
B. 'The lift'.

patient is in such a position that he will now have to turn his left hand round to continue his upward push. It sometimes helps if the rescuer can paddle in towards the patient as he pulls himself upwards. The rescuer must lose no time in getting over to his patient, but the last yard must be careful and controlled. When practising this in a pool, it is as well to wear a crash helmet, just in case someone is over enthusiastic.

Eskimo Side Rescue

The side rescue is by far the more useful Eskimo method. If someone capsizes in front of you, paddle fast, and as you come alongside the upturned boat, without slowing down, grasp the nearest wrist of the patient tightly, and as your canoe loses momentum with the drag of the other, place his hand on your paddle loom (Figure 52A). Your man then brings his other hand round underneath to hold your loom and pulls himself to the surface (Figure 52B). The man in the illustration will have to change the grip with his right hand to finish off his push into the upright position. It is important that the rescuer place the nearest hand on the paddle loom; otherwise the capsized man may well grab the loom on the wrong side. An hysterical little scene is then enacted as our hero tries to pull himself up on the wrong side, usually to no avail, while the rescuer tries as calmly as possible to inform the man, still underwater of course, that he wants to be up on the other side. The man being rescued must have sufficient control and air not to clutch in desperation the first thing his hand touches. Grasping the rescuer's wrist in a vice-like death clutch doesn't help anybody.

The joy of the side rescue is that it can be done quickly. Even if the rescuer is approaching from a position at right angles to the upturned boat, he can always turn at the last minute and execute a side rescue rather than a bow rescue, thus minimising the chance of holing a boat.

DEEP WATER RESCUES

A man in the water with an upturned canoe beside him presents an entirely different rescue situation. Over the years, various methods

Figure 53. HI deep water rescue.
A. Positioning of upturned canoe.   B. Emptying the canoe.
C. Rear deck method of re-entry.

of deep water rescues involving emptying and re-entering a capsized canoe have been devised, tried and tested. Some have been
rejected out of hand as being far too complicated, while others
failed in rough conditions.

One called the H rescue was popular for many years. The
upturned canoe was lifted and emptied while being held at either
end by the rescuers, their canoe being parallel to each other, and
the boat to be emptied at right angles to them. In choppy or windy
conditions, paddles went astray, the rescuers were unsupported,
and the canoes drifted together, putting the men in a very unstable position while they were still holding the canoe in the air. I
have not included this rescue as its use is so limited.

HI Rescue

The most successful rescue in really rough conditions is the HI
(so called because of the position adopted by the canoes), also
known as the Ipswich. During the rescue the paddles are under
control, the canoes form a close raft giving stability, and the man in
the water, besides being able to help considerably with the rescue,
need never lose contact with the rescue canoes. The rescuing
canoeists position themselves at either side of the upturned bow
about a yard apart, facing into the swell. The three paddles
forming a bridge across the canoes, the bow of the upturned boat
is lifted high so that the cockpit clears the water (Figure 53A).

Helped by the man in the water, the canoe is then fed backwards
over the paddles and rested on its cockpit coaming, where it can
be seesawed by the rescuers, assisted by the man in the water who
supports himself on one of the bows while pushing upwards and
then pulling down, all in time with the swell, and thus emptying
the canoe (Figure 53B).

The canoe is turned the right way up, put onto the water,
pushed forwards, then back under the paddles into the re-entry
raft position. To execute a rear deck re-entry, the paddles can be
kept across the boats or pushed out of the way. The positions of the
rescuers' arms are also variable. They can be as in Figure 53C or
they can be crossed over each other, one hand of each man grasping
the opposite side of the cockpit coaming, thus making a stronger
link. Practice will help the individual decide which is best.

The patient comes between his own canoe and one of the rescuing canoes, places his hands on the apex of both decks—his afterdeck and the other foredeck—and hoists himself upwards so that he is eventually sitting straddled on the rear deck of his own canoe. He then shunts himself forwards and into the cockpit. The rescuers keep supporting the raft until the spray cover is firmly secured.

From the positioning of the canoes to the finish of the rescue should take about one minute during practice on calm water. I practice this in a swimming pool, creating artificial waves by tossing a canoe up and down in the shallow end, while helpers splash with paddles all around the deep end and the odd sadist throws buckets of water over the participants for added realism.

Some points to remember:

1. Be quick! The man in the water may freeze.
2. It is better to lift the bow first, because there should be more buoyancy in the back half of the canoe. For all methods of rescue *the canoe must be full of buoyancy*. I was going to go on and say that if you *did* have inadequate buoyancy, you deserve all you get, but unfortunately someone else gets it. *You* won't have the job of lifting your own waterlogged canoe, although you will have to spend much longer freezing to death in the water while someone else does the struggling.
3. The man in the water must at no time lose contact with the rescue group if conditions are windy. His canoe and the two rescue canoes can be blown away faster than he can swim after them. So *hang on to at least one canoe at all times*.
4. Re-entry can sometimes be a problem.

The man in the water must remember to tuck his spray cover out of the way before hoisting himself up onto his rear deck. A rear deck carrying equipment, together with all the attendant elastics, ropes and hooks, can present a man whose legs are straddled across a flat Eskimo deck with untold problems as he tries to hitch himself forwards towards the cockpit.

Considerable strain is sometimes placed on the rescuers' arms when the patient raises himself from the water onto the back deck. A system I have developed using the paddles to give support for a side entry is much more satisfactory. See Figure 57.

Figure 54. Rafted T deep water rescue.
A. Lifting the canoe.
B. Emptying the canoe.

Rafted T and Single T Rescues

The rescue canoes raft up together. The paddles can either be in the paddle park or sandwiched between the two close canoes. With the upturned canoe at right angles to the two-man raft, the bow is quickly lifted high in the air to clear the cockpit of the water, in order to get as little water into the canoe as possible. It is then fed across the foredecks of the canoes. The man in the water can assist in the rescue by swimming around to one side and reaching high into the air to pull the bow of the canoe downwards (Figure 54A) to help drain the canoe.

After the canoe has been emptied, it is turned the right way up. Re-entry can be either along the rear deck as previously described, or from the side in a manner similar to Figure 56C, except that the paddle is supported by the rescuers sitting in their canoes. The method is shown in Figure 57.

In this method of rescue, the strain on the canoe decks, usually more than they can stand, causes them to smash to bits, not to mention the fact that sandwiching the front of the spray cover between the sharp edge of the cockpit coaming and the canoe across the deck can succeed in slicing it quite neatly. During the emptying action of the rescuing canoeists, our man in the water can be left in a very vulnerable position out on his own away from the raft. Thus, because of the difficulty of lifting the capsized canoe full of water, because of the damage caused to equipment and because of the 'way out' position of the man in the water if he tries to help, this can be considered only a good second to the HI rescue.

The chief merit of this method lies in the fact that emptying and righting a canoe this way can be done by one man if necessary, when it becomes the single T rescue. If the single T rescuer has difficulty in lifting and tilting the canoe, he can lean right over onto the opposite side, holding onto the 'rescued' canoe until the end goes down and the water swills down to that end. Because it can be done by one man and can be done extremely fast, ability to carry out the single T rescue is a must for anyone who is going to lead or be responsible for groups of people on open water.

If, and I repeat, *if* a rescue must be done within the surf line, 'rafted' rescues are not a good proposition because escape from

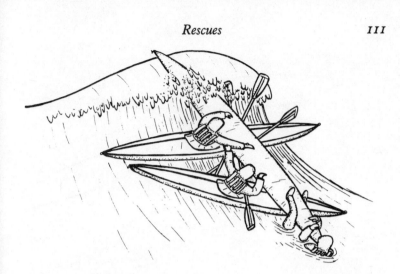

Figure 55. Things can go sadly wrong when rescues are attempted inside the surf line.

paddles, partner and patient's boat is a slow process. With the single T rescue, however, if the rescuer sees a large breaking wave approaching he can throw the upturned canoe off his foredeck quickly and look after himself. Rafted rescues done within the surf line, although providing endless entertainment for onlookers on the beach, rarely have more than a 50% chance of success (Figure 55). At best the rescuers will have many tense moments, at worst, damaged boats and serious injury.

If a capsize occurs within the surf line, entailing a long and dangerous swim ashore, it is best to tow man and upturned canoe farther out to sea and perform a rescue away from the breakers.

All-in Rescue

Perhaps one of the worst situations any canoeist can find himself in is when all the canoeists are in the water, with no one upright to perform a rescue. This can easily happen in a sudden unexpected squall.

First of all, collect your wits, then the paddles and canoes. Secure the paddles into the paddle parks or deck elastics. Notice in

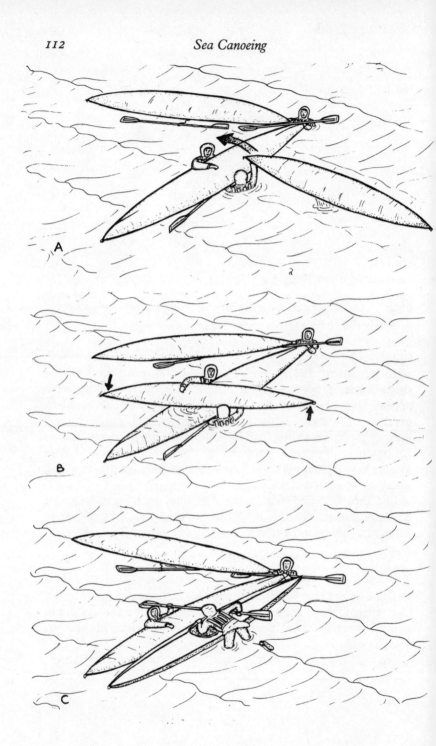

A

B

C

Figure 56A that the group is all together and that no one can get left behind by the raft's blowing away at high speeds. If you're going anywhere, you'll all go together.

The delicate part of the whole operation is emptying the first canoe without losing the air trapped in the canoe that is to be used as a pivot. Trying this with canoes *having no buoyancy at all* (in a swimming pool of course), I devised a system which is successful. While one man, holding the spare canoe, supports either the bow or stern, the two men amidships hold one hand each onto the cockpit coaming underneath the canoe. This prevents the boat's tipping sideways and losing the supporting air trapped inside. As shown in Figure 56B, with his right hand the nearest man lifts the bow of the canoe as high as possible into the air, the cockpit clear of the water. Retaining the grip on the coaming with his left hand, he feeds or throws the upturned canoe across to his partner. Then, with the pivot canoe underneath kept as steady and as level as possible, the top canoe can be seesawed carefully and emptied.

Most of the tests I have done have been with canoes having no buoyancy so that any tilting of the pivot canoe caused it to fill and sink. Thus with canoes even moderately full of buoyancy the rescues can be completed quickly.

Once the first canoe is emptied, the problem arises as to how to get in it without filling the canoe used as a pivot. A bridge is formed with a paddle across the two canoes (Figure 56C). Our man in the water on the far side supports an end of the paddle with one hand while he rests the other on the upturned hull or holds on to the coaming underneath. The nearest man puts his weight onto the paddle and pulls himself up and into the cockpit. Any pressure on the pivot canoe is counteracted by the support man.

The rescue can then continue by methods laid out in earlier rescues.

Figure 56. All-in deep water rescue.
A. Method of placing first canoe for emptying.
B. Emptying first canoe.
C. Method of re-entry into first canoe.

H

Figure 57. Side method of re-entry.

Members of the British Canoe Union's coaching scheme should be able to take charge of any of the rescues described and if necessary from a position actually in the water. They should also be able to empty a canoe unassisted, a deed they may have to do more than once when leading novice expeditions.

Over the years, I have been obliged to encourage students to experiment with many types of re-entry to meet the needs of various circumstances and differing abilities. In doing so I have been forced to listen to chaotic crashes and thuds, screams of agony and plaintive pleas, especially from fragile young misses, that arms were simply not strong enough. Finally, in desperation, I developed a method of a side re-entry needing so little effort on the part of the rescuer that a third canoe is unnecessary. The man in Figure 57 could easily let go of the cockpit coaming with his right hand and grasp the seat of the patient's pants or the bottom of his buoyancy aid and assist him into the cockpit if necessary. All the weight is on the paddle loom where it touches the deck, not on the rescuer's arm. The rescuer may feel simply an upward pressure under his armpit.

The man in the water hoists himself up by placing his left hand at the centre rear of the cockpit coaming, the other hand on the paddle loom. He then pulls himself upwards, placing his behind squarely over the cockpit, after executing a neat half turn to the right.

Figure 58. Repairing a leaking canoe. It has been discovered that the canoe is leaking. The two experienced canoeists are well out to sea. The man from the damaged boat sits tandem on the other canoe, sculling the paddle backwards and forwards to steady the rescue canoe. The leaking boat is hoisted across the rescue canoe, cockpit uppermost. It is then turned over and emptied. If the leak is only small or very gradual, the boat can be righted and the trip continued. However, if necessary, a repair kit can be taken from the damaged boat by the rescuer, or from behind his cockpit by the man sitting tandem. The repair can then be carried out by drying the boat and sealing it with broad tape. The rescuer's paddle is trapped against his hull by the patient's leg or placed in a paddle park. If two canoes participate in this rescue the patient will get only the bottom of his legs wet. If there are more canoes involved he can lie across the decks and keep completely dry. I have seen this operation performed successfully by an experienced coach, repairing his own boat while sitting on the foredeck of the rescue craft facing a very inexperienced rescuer, who did the support sculling. The emptying with the rear deck tandem can be done in very rough conditions and in high winds.

JUST BEFORE THE FLARE

The seas are very rough, and for some reason you have been separated from your companions. You have capsized in rough water and have failed to roll. You are in the water far from land. This situation should never arise but situations that *should* never arise have an ugly habit of doing so. Two alternatives are open to you:

The first possibility—Face the rear of the upturned canoe, one arm stretched out underneath the cockpit grasping the coaming at the far side, together with the paddle. The near hand also grasps the cockpit coaming. Steady the boat, take a deep breath and submerge. Still grasping the coaming and paddle, curl up your legs, drop your head down and let your legs enter the cockpit as part of a reverse somersault. If you have practised this at your local baths course you should now be able to roll up. Then holding the canoe steady and doing a sculling stroke with one hand, the other end of the paddle resting on the shoulder, start mopping the water out with your sponge or bailer. If you capsize in an overfall or tide race it may be necessary to wait while you drift clear of the rough water before trying this re-entry technique.

The second possibility—If you can't get back in, keep contact with the upturned canoe at all costs. You should leave the canoe only if you are absolutely certain you can swim to shore, because your chances of being seen in rough whitetopped seas are very slim. Your orange spray cover and most of your colourful lifejacket or buoyancy aid are under water out of sight and unless you happen to be wearing a vivid crash helmet, you will never be spotted. Fasten your orange paddles into the paddle park, undo one of the deck lines and tie it round your waist. You can send up a star shell —this is what you carry them for—and if need be, attract attention by waving the paddle to and fro in the air or by taking your large orange polythene exposure bag out of its case and allowing the wind to fill it (Figure 59). This bag can be seen on the water at a considerable distance. The fluorescent orange skull-caps worn by beach lifeguards could well be an added item in anyone's survival kit.

If you expect a long period of immersion and you are not wearing a wet-suit, you might climb inside the exposure bag. Obviously

Figure 59. A bad day. The lifejacket comes into its own in conditions such as this, as once it is inflated, the man can keep still, perhaps even sleep. Even when unconscious, he has a chance of not drowning. However, unless adequately clothed, he will not long survive the cold. His orange exposure bag, filled with wind, his orange paddle blades, perhaps even his orange spray cover tied to the end of his paddle, will all help him to be seen by rescuers.

water will get into it, but the top of the bag can be pulled well up around your neck or even up over your head, while one hand still holds onto the canoe. Curl up and lie back on your lifejacket. Any water that enters the bag will become still. You may be surprised how much warmer you will be inside the wet bag than in water that is continually changing round your body!

While carrying out any of the methods of attracting attention, don't thrash about. Keep your arms near your sides if you can and cross your legs, thus preventing loss of vital body heat from your armpits and crutch. Above all, keep calm. You will live longer: fear can accelerate and intensify hypothermia and shock.

The planned use of rescue or accompanying boats for canoe expeditions is alien to the dedicated sea canoeist. Sea canoeing with a safety boat is rather like climbing a rock face with a large rope net strung a few yards underneath: suddenly *any* climb becomes possible. Two occasions, however, come to mind when safety boats are possibly acceptable: crossings of the English Channel, where the volume of shipping traffic is such that the safety factor is taken completely out of the hands of the canoeist, and outdoor centres, where young novices are given a feeling of adventure by being taken on short sea trips and a feeling of safety in the knowledge that help is within hailing distance if needed in a hurry. It must also be borne in mind that all rescue boats are not reliable. I have known more than one accompanied trip where the rescue craft either broke down or was unable to cope with the prevailing sea conditions, thus endangering not only the lives of its crew but also the lives of the canoeists they were supposed to protect.

5

Waves

During all your happy years of sea canoeing, waves of one kind or another will be your constant companion, so that every canoeist should know something about the waves he is likely to meet—or which are likely to meet him. By looking at a map or chart and equating certain coastal features, such as depth and shape of the sea bottom, with certain weather conditions it is possible to anticipate roughly the type and character of the wave you will meet, even if you cannot foretell its size and ferocity. Looking at a chart and noting the various submarine gradients make it possible to know whether a certain beach will be suitable for different kinds

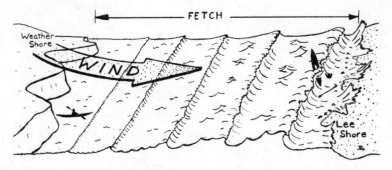

Figure 60. Fetch.
To the canoeist sheltering in the LEE of the cliffs, wind and water conditions appear suitable for the trip to the island. However, conditions in the open sea are quite different and a landing may be impossible.

119

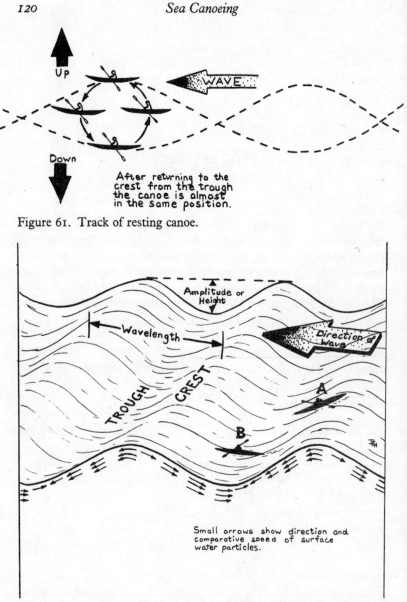

Figure 61. Track of resting canoe.

Figure 62. Formation of unbroken sea waves. Canoeist A is almost surfing down the face of the wave while canoeist B is retarded in the trough. This is the dreaded following sea of the novice. The wave will catch up to B and throw him forward. This type of following sea is a godsend for the experienced canoeist on a long sea trip, although surfing may be required at the end of the journey.

of canoe activities—that is, will you be able to surf, will you be able to land at all, will the surf be dangerous?

Waves are caused by the wind. All waves have two things in common: a crest, the highest part, and a trough, the lowest part. 'Soup' is the name given to the wave after it breaks.

Wind moving across still water immediately produces ripples, which are the smallest waves, with only a split second between one crest and another. Wind blowing across water flowing at the same speed will produce no waves, and wind blowing against the tidal stream produces steep standing waves.

The expanse of water the wind blows over, the amount of time it blows and the speed with which it blows all influence the size of the wave. The unobstructed distance over which the wind travels creating waves is *fetch* (Figure 60), and the greater the distance of fetch, the more opportunity the wind has to create larger, more powerful waves. Some waves travel faster than others, and as they move along across the oceans for hundreds, sometimes thousands, of miles, other wave patterns join them on their journey. It is little wonder that the sea often looks confused.

Storms hundreds of miles away will create a swell and it is this undulating movement of the sea which, when it reaches our coasts, causes surf to break on our beaches and pound on our rocks. Although the swell or wave moves a stationary canoe up and down,

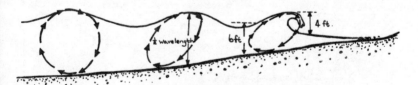

Normal circular orbital movement of wave particles before wave reaches shallow water.

Orbital movement begins to become elliptical as the wave approaches shallow water. This is caused by the frictional resistance or bottom drag, and usually occurs when the depth is ½ the wavelength

When the depth is approximately 1½ times the wave height, the wave begins to break.

Figure 63. Orbital movement of wave particles.

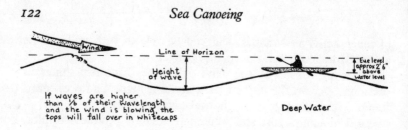

Line of Horizon

Height
of wave

Wind

Eye level
approx 2' 6"
above
water level

If waves are higher
than ⅛ of their wavelength
and the wind is blowing, the
tops will fall over in whitecaps

Deep Water

Figure 64. Canoeist judging height of wave.

the relative position of the canoe on the surface of the water alters
very little (Figure 61).

Notice the orbital movement of the water particles. When the
canoe is paddled and moves forwards, the surface movement of the
water particles has a definite influence on its progress (Figure 63).
Long undulating swells hold no danger for a canoe, but if the wind
blows strong enough and the height of the waves gets higher than
$\frac{1}{8}$ of their wavelength, the tops fall over themselves, forming
whitecaps.

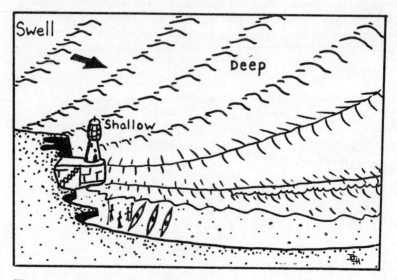

Swell

Deep

Shallow

Figure 65. Wave refraction off a point.

When the canoeist is out at sea in a swell and perhaps in a high state of tension, it is sometimes difficult to judge the height of the waves. Remember that when you are on top of a crest, the other crest, the height of which you are trying to estimate, may be on its way down again. Waves tend to look much larger and more menacing when viewed from the trough (Figure 64).

As I have mentioned, water particles move with a circular motion. As a wave reaches shallow water it slows down, and when it gets into water $1\frac{1}{2}$ times its height (called its critical depth), the frictional resistance caused by the bottom makes the crest topple over, producing a broken wave (Figure 63).

Figure 66. Wave refraction around an island.

Figure 67. Reflected waves. Waves strike the pier and are reflected back; these superimpose themselves on the original wave pattern. The trough of one may be cancelled out by the crest of another, or if a crest meets a crest, the wave height will be higher. The crashing together of the two wave patterns producing a high vertical broken wave is called clapotis. This type of area offers an exciting and challenging playground for experienced and skilful canoeists. With care the waves along the side of the pier can be surfed, but obviously this can prove hazardous.

Figure 65 shows how the swell rolling in parallel to itself is slowed down near the shore while the outside of the swell marches on at its original speed, producing what is called a *refraction curve*. This refraction gives canoeists and board surfers the graduated surf suitable for experts and beginners alike and also the breaking 'shoulder' which is the delight of surf canoe paddlers. Conditions like these are found in Beadnell Bay in Northumberland, where a huge north-easterly or easterly swell runs, and also in parts of Wales and the south-west coast.

When you paddle out from a piered harbour, remember that the swell which does not affect you whilst you are in the sheltered area between the piers is quite a different matter when you reach exposed water around the piers and beyond. This is because waves

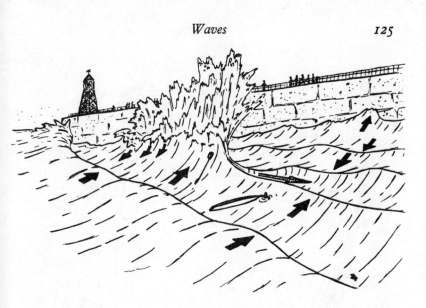

Figure 68. Reflected waves and clapotis. If the angle is acute where the reflected wave meets the original wave pattern, and if a big swell is running, the resulting clapotis can be tremendously powerful. The two toppling walls of water will collide almost head on, sending tons of water vertically skywards in a thundering plume that rushes along like an express train. This is *not* a safe area in which to canoe, and the capsized paddler in the illustration is in a bad position. With his canoe and paddle, he must swim seawards clear of the 'break' area. His companions can then give him a rescue outside the danger area, where he should never have been in the first place.

are reflected from piers and cliffs, and as will be apparent from Figures 67 and 68, the crashing together of two wave patterns can produce the haystack effect of *clapotis*. *Clapotis* can also be produced by waves being refracted around an island (Figure 66).

A dumping wave, depicted in Figure 69, is caused by a steeply shelving bottom. The wave reaches its critical depth quickly, peaks up and breaks suddenly, dragging with it sand and small stones, which rise up inside the curl. Then wave and stones crash down with tremendous impact, smashing canoes, filling eyes and ears and sand-blasting the battered canoeist. The breaking of the wave is almost explosive, because the air trapped and compressed inside

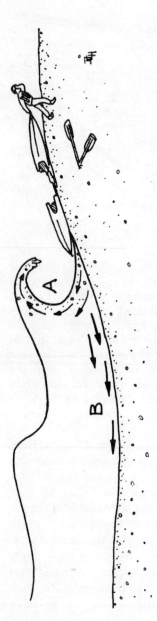

Figure 69. Dumping wave. Air is trapped at A as wave breaks. Note the water draining back out to sea at B. This is the undertow.

Figure 70. Storm water waves. A and B show the area of primary break, where the waves are breaking quarter to half a mile out to sea, creating a powerful undertow more associated with inshore 'dumpers'. In normal water conditions, the presence of the shallower water at A and B would remain unknown. C marks the area of secondary break, and provides a dangerous playground for canoeists. (not to scale)

the breaking curl exerts tremendous pressure. This is undoubtedly a most dangerous type of wave. Landings and departures through such waters should be made with extreme caution.

More deadly than shore dumping waves are the waves of storm water shown in Figure 70. These are huge, pounding, crashing waves whose area of breaking extends far out to sea. Occasionally, some parallel order of approach can be noticed in the waves but mainly the pattern is confused. Close in shore at C the surf may look manageable for canoeing. I shall call this the secondary break area. But even the inshore 'soup' here generates power tremendous enough to capsize and inhibit rolling. The man and boat can be forced backwards as he tries to paddle out, his canoe stabbing viciously into the sand with a back-breaking jerk. The man may roll up and find he is under water. Viewed from the level of the beach, the primary break at A and B may be hardly visible as the picture has a foreshortened look with the waves appearing to pile one on top of the other. Only by climbing higher up the beach can one obtain a better view of the whole situation. The primary break is the area of the fearsome dumping, deep water waves which because of their great height now break over depths which would normally have no influence on the surface swell.

Each of these deep water dumping waves forms its own dreadful undertow. Rescue in this area is very difficult, if not impossible.

Figure 71. Surfing wave. As the wave breaks, it tumbles over from the top and rolls down the slope. For the whole of its life cycle this is the finest form of surfing wave. Both the breaking wave and the 'soup' it creates lack the violence of the dumper or the storm water waves.

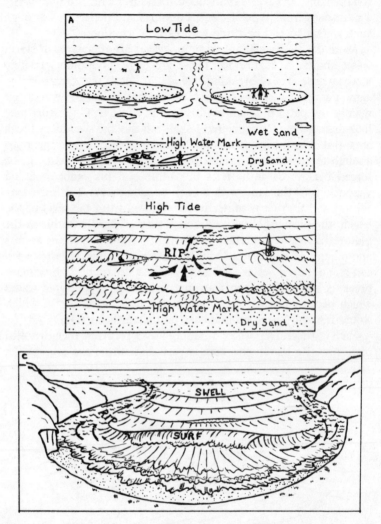

Figure 72. Wave refraction and rips in a bay. When surfing in a bay (B) use the surf in the centre; then use the rip as a quick and easy way out again. The swell refraction is caused by the sides of the bay.

Storm water is not for recreational canoeing and should be avoided, and even the secondary break should be treated with great caution.

The type of wave which surf canoeists travel many miles to use is shown in Figure 71. These waves can be very large, but because of their shape and because the break topples gently over from the top they are quite manageable. Found on beaches which have a long, even, gradual slope, these surfing waves do not usually have an undertow.

Rip is a phenomenon consisting of movement of water at a different speed from that of the surrounding water.

Water which has come ashore as surf is taken back out to sea by *rips* as shown in Figure 72. On the beach at low tide, deep channels may be seen. At high tide these channels form rips taking water back out to sea in large volumes at 1 or 2 knots, faster than you can tow a canoe back to shore if you capsize one. Rip channels, which provide a swift means of getting out through surf, can also be found at the sides of bays. (Figure 72B).

It is almost impossible for a swimmer, from his position at water level, to know that he is in a rip. If you are in a canoe and are able to see the rip, you should give him directions to get out of it.

I

6
Winds and Weather

As far as the sea canoeist is concerned, for weather read wind. Rain, sleet, hail, fog—all these are water off a canoeist's back, but wind is a different matter. It is the whistling, tearing, shrieking wind that grasps at the fluttering, jerking paddle blades. Flying spray fills smarting eyes and lashes the face. It drains the strength gradually at first; then, as realisation comes that progress forwards is almost nil, demoralisation and the seeming futility of the fight take away the will to go on. Arms that are still physically strong suddenly feel weak. The canoe becomes almost impossible to turn. The discovery is made that the constant crashing of the sea over the bow and along the deck, is gradually filling the canoe, finding its way through the spray cover, which is impossible to remove in these conditions to mop out. Body heat just seems to be snatched away. If ever sea canoeing had an enemy, the wind is it.

Winds do not arrive from nowhere, and we can be reasonably prepared. The following are useful aids:

1. A radio weather forecast.
2. A knowledge of clouds and weather lore.
3. A check of the barometer.
4. Bad weather cones outside the coastguard station.
5. A phone call to the local weather centre or coastguard station.
6. A knowledge of previous weather conditions for the time of year.
7. Intuition.

CLOUDS

Cirrus Fibrous and feather-like, these are the highest clouds of all. They herald the approach of a Frontal Weather System and are sometimes called 'Mares' Tails'. If they are arranged in a haphazard manner or if they start to dissolve, fine weather is indicated. However, if in parallel streaks feathering up at the ends, this probably means high winds, blowing in the direction of the streaks.

Cirro cumulus Cirro cumulus are spread over the sky like the ripples in wet sand on the beach. They cast no shadows and are usually an indication of fine weather, but the wind could be strong. This type of cloud, nicknamed the 'Mackerel Sky', is associated with the cirrus cloud in that both are very high and both indicate the approach of a Front.

Cirro stratus This is a milky white sheet covering the whole sky. The sun shines through very weakly, while the moon will have a halo.

Alto cumulus These appear in isolated formations of waves or lines and are rather like the 'Mackerel Sky' in appearance, although lower. They are a light or medium grey colour depending on the direction of the sun. When the cloud is castellated—i.e. piled upwards in a castle-like structure—this could mean thunder.

Alto stratus Forming an even grey cloud sheet covering the sky, these tend to give the sun a dilute watery appearance.

Strato cumulus These big, soft, grey clouds give an overcast effect. The weather should be dry and settled.

Stratus This is an even layer of cloud, really a high fog. The weather will be mild, warm and damp.

Nimbus These are big, black, rain clouds, ominous in appearance. As nimbo stratus they form a heavy layer of rain cloud.

Cumulus These huge white clouds are like giant balls of cotton wool. Fracto cumulus, small broken clouds, mean fair summer weather.

Cumulo nimbus These are very high mountainous clouds. The summit of the towering mass often forms itself into an anvil top, which is the classic shape for a bad-weather thunder cloud.

Here are some more visual signs in the sky:

If clouds start and get lower, it means bad weather is coming.

If you see the rising sun breaking above a bank of clouds, beware of wind.

If the clouds at sunrise have a nasty purple look, it is going to be stormy and windy.

When the sun sets in a copper sky—bright yellow—look out for wind.

A halo around the moon or sun after a fine spell means wind.

If the clouds high up are moving in a different direction from those lower down, or in a different direction from the wind at ground level, the wind is going to change in their direction.

SQUALLS

Wind speeds given in weather forecasts refer to the average sustained wind speed, not to gusts, which can take the form of squalls. A squall is a brief, violent windstorm, usually with rain, hail or snow. When a squall is stretched across the sky, heralding the approach of a cold front, it is called a line squall, which should not be confused with the isolated squall cloud (Figure 73). To give a violent downdraught these clouds must have a considerable development vertically. If the squall cloud is above you, the heavy cold air can rush out of the cloud in one almighty initial blast, which can capsize a whole group of unprepared canoeists. This is the squall front.

I remember being about a mile off Holy Island, Northumberland, watching a squall approaching. The breeze was soon livened by a few outriding gusts. The sea seemed to be tumbling and falling towards us. Then suddenly there was a howling, streaming wind and white tops all around. The raindrops were so close together that sea and sky seemed to be one. The paddler in front of me was outlined by the spray bouncing off his head, shoulders and canoe. We seemed to be beaten down as we leaned on what appeared to be a solid wall of wind, sea spray and rain. Suddenly it started to ease, the drops of rain seemed smaller. I could lift my head up and see again. In a matter of minutes it had gone as swiftly as it came and we watched the ominous wall of rain retreat

Figure 73. Squall cloud. Updraughts can travel at 100 ft. per second.

into the distance. If you can brace yourself and warn your group to prepare themselves, once the violent blast is over the rest is almost an anti-climax. Continuous squalls however can upset a planned journey.

WEATHER CHART

The weather chart in Figure 74 is based on monthly surveys over a period of 100 years. It could be called the historic system of weather prediction. There are variations in the weather, but on average, certain weather conditions occur again and again. Reading this chart may well give some indication of what you might expect when planning trips and expeditions months in advance.

Figure 74.	WEATHER CHART
January	Violent storms. Low pressure with high winds can build up huge seas. Good canoe-building weather.
February	Bad weather. Hail and snow. Varnish some paddles. Visit the National Canoe Exhibition.
March 1-10	'Many weathers'. Storms and gales. This is the stormiest period in Britain. Canoeists in the north and in Scotland face much stronger winds than in the south.
10-20	Much less stormy. Sometimes very fine with settled conditions.
21-31	Storms and gales. Low temperatures. Possibility of snow, so try the ski slopes.
April 1-15	Unsettled weather. Moderate storms and gales. Prevailing winds are W/NW.
16-22	The season of the 'anvil top' thunder cloud, although it can be bright and sunny.
23-30	Unsettled weather again, perhaps snow, sometimes the odd gale.
May 1-10	Slightly higher temperatures. There can be some cold winds, usually from the N/W, and the occasional night frost. So into the loft and check the camping gear.
11-22	Usually a cold period. Winds can be strong from the north.
23-31	A little warmer. The winds have dropped, but this time of May has produced some heavy thunderstorms with flooding. Good for river canoeists.
June 1-10	Changeable and cool, but the weather starts to improve towards the 10th.
11-30	Usually fine and warm, sometimes very hot. Don't forget the dark glasses and the sun cream. Watch out for thunderstorms, and perhaps a squall.
July 1-7	Rather unsettled showers and thunderstorms.
8-21	Good chance of hot weather. Watch out for sea fogs during humid spells. Light or moderate southerly winds. Odd thunderstorms.
22-31	Unsettled.
August 1-7	Still unsettled and a little cooler.
8-15	Warmer again and more settled. About this time

	we get the most sunshine and the highest temperatures, especially in the south-east. Sunburn and fog are both dangers.
16-31	Still warm, but there can be thunderstorms.
September 1-14	Dry settled weather (now that we are back at work).
15-30	Can be stormy with strong winds from the N/W. Enrol now for that canoeing bath course.
October 1-7	Campers, this is the wettest month of the year. It can be very stormy. Low pressure systems keep travelling across the country from the west. Temperatures start to fall noticeably.
8-21	Settled conditions can prevail about this time as we know to our cost from various N/E Canoe Surfing Championships.
22-31	Long periods of storms.
November 1-7	. . . And more storms: one depression after another. Plenty of rain.
8-21	Settled weather, but it's cold now. In the morning you'll have to jump on your buoyancy aid to soften the ice inside before putting it on. Watch out for that cold sea fog.
22-30	Storms and winds (these can be almost guaranteed for your advanced sea course) usually come from the N/W or north, with of course the odd N/E gale.
December	Usually gets a little warmer at the beginning of the month, but gets colder and stormier as the month goes on.

THE BAROMETER

Make a habit of checking your barometer. I was brought up in a house where the barometer was tapped every morning and evening. It gives an instant indication of air pressure, so let us see what happens when you observe it.

Starts to rise. If it starts to rise after being well below its normal for the time of year, the first part of the rise may well bring very strong winds or severe gales from the north. If it keeps on rising it will bring fair weather.

A quick rise means the good weather may not last and the wind may come from the north.

A steady rise means good weather is on its way. High pressure brings an anti-cyclone, which means good weather is here and is going to continue. Light winds blow in a clockwise direction. During the summer months, the anti-cyclone brings hot fine weather with very little cloud. In winter, the still air brings fog and frost.

A quick fall means a storm is on its way, so don't go far off shore.

A steady fall means bad weather is on its way but taking its time.

A fall while a southerly wind is freshening and backing to the south-east means the wind could veer and produce a westerly gale.

A fall while south-easterly winds are blowing could bring a gale. However, south-easterly gales do not last long.

A fall during south-easterly winds while the temperature starts to increase could make the wind veer to the south and south-west.

A fall while the wind is backing to the south and south-west is a sure sign of bad weather.

Constant low pressure brings unstable and changeable weather with thick, heavy clouds, gales and storms, and big swells. This is a depression, which we in Britain know and love so well. These low pressure systems travel very quickly.

BEAUFORT WIND SCALE

When we left the world of Fahrenheit and started measuring temperature by Centigrade, it was all very confusing. Tell me the temperature is going to be 40°F., and I know what I'm going to take when I go canoeing. But if told I'm going to experience 20°C., I know not whether I am going to sweat or shiver. In the same way, I am one of those people who were brought up on the Beaufort Wind Scale. If I hear that a Force 6 is due, I know exactly what the wind will feel like on my face, and what it will do to the water and the canoe. But if I am told that the wind will be blowing at 30 m.p.h., I honestly don't know what it means until I convert it to Beaufort. So for poor mortals like me, here is the Beaufort Wind Scale, modified somewhat for the canoeist.

Figure 75.   BEAUFORT WIND SCALE

Beaufort No.	Speed in m.p.h.	Term	Grading	Conditions (these depend on whether wind is on- or off-shore or sheltered)
0	0	Calm		A nice quiet paddle is indicated. Do some fishing; spear a few flat fish. Long trips by coracle possible.
1	1-3	Light air	Very easy	A few ripples. Still good for fishing. Take the open Canadian out.
2	4-6	Light breeze	Easy	Feel wind on face; little wavelets. Take the Canadian back in.
3	7-11	Gentle breeze	Fairly easy	A few scattered whitetops. Flag flutters straight out on coastguard station.
4	12-16	Mod. breeze	Moderate	Proficiency standard should start for sheltered water unless an onshore breeze.
5	17-21	Fresh breeze	Moderately difficult	Lots of whitetops. It's hard work into the wind for the inexperienced. Proficiency standard tackle this only in sheltered water or near shore.
6	22-28	Strong breeze	Difficult	Rescues will be difficult. Warnings issued to small craft. Seas getting big; whitetops and spray. Proficiency man will be in trouble.
7	29-35	Mod. gale	Very difficult	You *must* be strong and experienced; your equipment should be good. Seas are big. Canoes difficult to turn.

BEAUFORT WIND SCALE (Continued)

Beaufort No.	Speed in m.p.h.	Term	Grading	Conditions (these depend on whether wind is on- or off-shore or sheltered)
				Very difficult to make headway. Wind catches at paddle blades. Foam is blown off in long white streaks, lots of spray. Communication very difficult.
8	36-43	Gale	Dangerous	Experienced man may handle this in sheltered water. In the open sea, men are extended almost to the limit. Seas are piling up and breaking continuously. Wind catches the canoe on the crests. It's a fight all the time. Communication almost impossible unless *very* experienced. Each man looks out for himself. Rescues impractical.
9	44-51	Strong gale	Extremely dangerous	Fight for survival in open sea. Huge, breaking, spume-swept waves, close together. *No rescues.* Communication—hand signals (if you can spare the hand). Try a prayer: I find these work.

The question of whether it is safe to venture out to sea does not entirely depend on wind speed, since the degree of danger or risk inherent in any wind speed can be heightened or lessened by the particular circumstances. The area being exposed, a large existing swell, the wind against the tide—all are factors that can increase the risk, which means that in some circumstances a Force 5 or 6 could be a foolhardy gamble for a canoeist with little advanced experience, whereas with a sheltered area, a flat sea roughened only by the high wind, and the wind blowing with the tide, even a Force 7 or 8 could be quite a reasonable proposition.

WEATHER FORECASTS

The late-night weather forecast on television is always worth watching. Radio, on the other hand, still provides the most widely used forecasts, because it keeps the listener informed at frequent intervals throughout the day. The times of shipping forecasts can be obtained from the *Radio Times* or from most newspapers.

These forecasts open with a short summary of general weather conditions. A forecast is given for each of the sea areas for the next 24 hours, including the direction and strength of the wind, visibility and general weather. After the forecast for the larger *sea* areas comes a similar one for the *coastal* areas (Figure 76), and the barometer pressure is given in addition to information as to whether it is rising or falling.

When the wind reaches over 40 knots, a gale warning is broadcast. The BBC helps us by interrupting its programmes as soon as the information is received. If a gale is

Imminent   it will arrive in 6 hours.
Soon   it will arrive in 6 to 12 hours.
Later   it will arrive in over 12 hours.

When a wind is said to be veering, it is changing direction in a clockwise manner. When it is said to be backing, it is changing direction in an anti-clockwise manner.

Certain newspapers such as *The Times, The Daily Telegraph, The Guardian* and *The Scotsman* give detailed weather forecasts, but these are obviously not as immediate as the radio. However, it might well be that while off the west coast of Scotland you find a battered but up-to-date copy of *The Scotsman*, when all you can

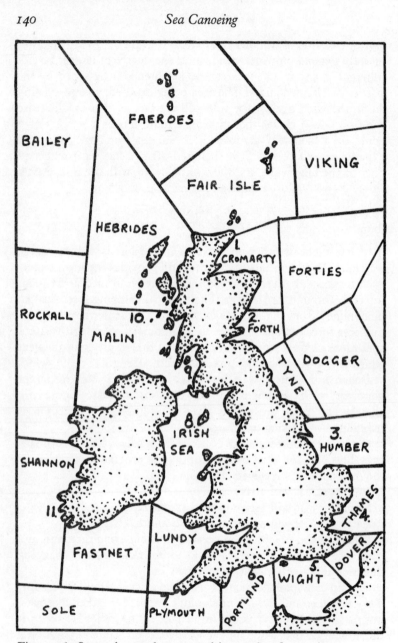

Figure 76. Sea and coastal areas used in weather forecasting.
Coastal areas:

1. Wick	5. Royal Sovereign	9. Prestwick
2. Bell Rock	6. Portland	10. Tiree
3. Dowsing	7. Scilly Isles	11. Valentia
4. Galloper	8. Ronaldsway	

get on your transistor are noises from outer space and the sound of some unidentified radio beacon, harmonising with high-speed morse.

LOCAL WEATHER CENTRES

Set up by the Meteorological Office, these centres are extremely helpful in giving local weather information, and they are usually conveniently located so that members of the public can read there at their leisure. In some areas the weather forecasts are pre-recorded, and by dialling the appropriate number, which can be found in the front pages of the telephone book, the canoeist can get an accurate, but rather impersonal, forecast.

THE COASTGUARD

The coastguard are always very co-operative and will give information over the telephone. Apart from the local weather and wind speed, they can also be relied upon to give the height of the swell, which often proves useful.

Do not forget that although the coastguard may tell you that your trip is ill advised when the weather is bad, they are not allowed officially to advise you that conditions are suitable for your trip. Thus if things go wrong—and they often do—the onus rests firmly on your shoulders, not theirs. Even the shoulders of the coastguard are not that broad.

When the coastguard advise against a particular trip because of prevailing weather conditions, they base this advice on a wealth of experience. Unfortunately they have no idea of the potential of a canoe in rough seas handled by a good kayak man. So while proficiency level canoeists would do well to take their advice and find a piece of sheltered water somewhere, advanced canoeists must fall back on their considerable personal experience, and considering all factors, together with the coastguard's advice, make their own decisions accordingly. Remember that the advice given by the coastguard is designed to keep you alive and to allow the lifeboat crews to carry on their normal daily occupations without interruption. They cannot be wrong, even if you spend your day languishing on the beach, wishing that you had gone out after all.

VISUAL GALE WARNINGS

These take the form of large black cones 3 ft. high and 3 ft. across the base. If you see what appears to be a black triangle hanging on a mast from a coastguard station, an RAF or naval base, harbour offices or the yard arm of a fishery protection vessel, you will know that a gale either is in progress or is due within the next 12 hours.

If the point of the triangle is upwards, then the gale is from any point in the north sector of the compass. Pointing downwards means the gale will be from any point in the south sector.

At night, three lights are hung on the cone to form the points of a triangle. These can be any colour, but are usually red. These lights are used by all authorities as part of their information to shipping.

INTUITION

There comes a time, after all the usual checks have been made with the weather centre, the coastguard and other forecasts, when the weather is still, the clouds betray nothing. You look up, sniff, suck your teeth and gaze about. A deep feeling of apprehension slows you down while the rest are gleefully preparing for the trip.

Take careful note of the feeling: either cancel the trip or, if you do go ahead, be mentally alert to the possibility of the worst happening. If it doesn't, you'll be all right, but if it does you'll be prepared.

7

Tides and Tidal Streams

Paddle your canoe on the largest lake in the world and if the wind doesn't blow the water will be calm. The big difference between the largest of great lakes and some small sea bay is this: the sea is a live, living thing; it does not need wind to make it violent, because its waters are continually in restless motion, in some places with quiet subtlety, in others with great speed and noise. Unlike the weather, however, the behaviour of water movements is much easier to predict. Any canoeist who has watched and studied water as it flows down a river, around rock and past obstructions on the bank should be able to apply his experience to the movements of the sea around our coastal areas. When a tidal stream surges around a headland or rushes between islands, its behaviour is almost the same, although on a larger scale, as that of water in a river.

Let us look at tides and their causes, at some of the sea conditions associated with them and at the resultant movements of the sea which are generally referred to as tidal streams. Very briefly, the moon acts like some huge magnet upon the earth. As the earth turns on its axis it draws the sea and gives the tides a rhythmic rise and fall. The moon pulls the water nearest it while the water on the opposite side of the earth also rises. Therefore *twice* a day every part of the world has a *high tide* and a *low tide*. When it is high tide on the eastern coast of North America it is low tide around the British Isles. When the tide is rising it is said to be flooding and when it goes down it is ebbing. There are approximately 6¼ hours between high and low water. If it is high tide at 07.00 hours one day, the following day it will be at 07.52, a difference of about 50 minutes each day.

Twice every month when the moon has its greatest influence on the earth's waters, a little after new moon and full moon, *spring tides* occur (please note twice a *month*, not twice every spring). Tides will rise higher and fall lower then, and tide races and over-falls are more violent. Tidal streams run faster, thus giving more help or offering more resistance to paddlers. The water will un-cover rocks and wrecks that are rarely seen, or flood the tiny area where you were going to stop for lunch.

Halfway between each spring tide, when the moon has its least effect on the oceans, we have what are called *neap tides*. Any epic crossings or expeditions are best planned to coincide with these.

Because the moon's track around the earth is elliptical, it is nearer the earth at certain times than at others. When nearest, it is said to be in *perigee;* when farthest away, in *apogee*. When it is in perigee at almost the same time as a spring tide, the highest and lowest tides and the fastest tidal streams will occur.

Because the coastline of the British Isles is so indented and broken, it is important to remember when planning expeditions that although the tide may be out where you are, it could well be that a few miles away the tide is still moving and has in fact some two or three hours to go before slack water occurs. There is also a lag between the time of high water at the mouth of an estuary and the time of high water 5 or 6 miles inland. Heavy rain and melting snows can also affect the time of the flood.

At high and low water the tide remains more or less still—that is, slack—for some little time, but in some places the water is never really slack. The rate falls off and the water then tends to flow at right angles to its original path. If the area is particularly bad, slack tides may create huge, uneasy upsurges and swirls as if the water is trying to decide what to do next. Anyone who has paddled over the position of the whirlpool in the Gulf of Corry-vreckan at high tide will have been much aware of this.

It is not the movement of the tide up and down the beach that most affects us as canoeists during our paddling, but the tidal streams caused by the enormous amount of water which pours around the northern tip of Scotland and up the English Channel to fill the North Sea. As the tide floods it increases in speed as it

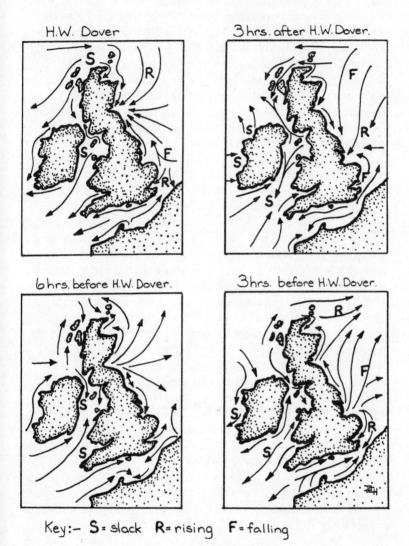

Key:– S = slack R = rising F = falling

Figure 77. Tidal streams around the British Isles.

forces it way between islands, swirling round headlands and emptying bays and estuaries. The narrower the gap between the pieces of land, the faster the tidal stream flows (Figure 77). This is particularly forcibly illustrated in the tides around the west coast of Scotland, with its islands, sea lochs and narrows where the flood rushes up one side of an island only to overtake a slower-moving tidal stream or collide with another fast tidal stream going in the opposite direction. Such complex tidal streams coupled with bad visibility and unstable weather make our coastal waters some of the most dangerous in the world to navigate.

A copy of the *Coastal Pilot* will give you all the information you need for specific pieces of water. For instance, if you wish to paddle across the Sound of Jura the *West Coast Pilot* will tell you the west-going stream begins +0410 HW Oban, which is some 28 miles to the north. You therefore add on 4 hr. 10 min. to Oban's HW time to find out when the west-going stream at the Sound of Jura begins, thus making the adjustment which is necessary to stop yourself being swept away in the wrong direction.

Let us suppose it is high slack and the tide is starting to ebb. At first the water moves slowly, then gathers speed until it is running at its fastest when it is halfway between high and low water, after which it gradually slows down again until it reaches low slack. The same speed change occurs when the tide starts to flood until it reaches high slack once more.

The speed of the tidal streams at any stage of the tide cycle can be estimated fairly accurately by the ratio 1:2:3:2:1. In rivers and estuaries the rate flow may not conform to the 1:2:3:2:1 rule and the water may be at its greatest speed soon after the tide has started to run. The rise and fall of the tide is sometimes worked out by applying the 1/12, 2/12, 3/12, 3/12, 2/12, 1/12 rule.

If a canoeist wishes to cross, for example, a mile-wide strait and the tide is running at more than 2 to 3 knots, he would do well to wait until the stream slackens off, thus saving himself a strenuous and prolonged ferry glide. It must be remembered that in any channel the water moves fastest at the centre. If the channel is several miles wide, as in Figure 78, it may be easier to leave point A while the tide is still running and arrive at the centre of the channel at slack water, and then to paddle on to B after the water has started to move again in the opposite direction. Because of the

Figure 78. Movement of water through a strait. The broad arrows indicate the fastest flowing water.

distance involved in long crossings such as the English Channel, it is difficult to work the tides successfully, so that any course line must be rather a dog-leg.

Along the south coast of England, tides can be very complex because when it is HW at one end of the Channel it is LW at the other. This can cause peculiar local conditions, such as the prolonged low-water condition at Portland known as the 'Gulder', or that at Southampton where the first flood rises normally for about 2 hours after LW, then rises very slowly (almost slack) for about 2 hours, after which the main flood tide runs for about 2¼ hours until HW. Then to complicate matters it falls a little for about an hour until it rises again for over an hour, creating another HW. So if you are canoeing in the Solent, get some local information from the Sea Canoeing Centre at Calshot or do your homework *well*.

If we know the time of high tide at a major port such as Dover, the time at which other parts of the coast will have high water in relation to it will always be the same, or remain constant. After reference to a table of tidal constants—a list of times which must be added to or subtracted from the high tide at Dover—it is easy to find out exactly what the tide is doing in a particular place at a particular time. Tidal constants are marked on the maps in the AA *Members' Handbook* and HW London Bridge and Dover are also given in *The Times* and *The Daily Telegraph*. (*See* Appendix 1.)

If the homework is not done properly for your trip you might find yourself arriving at your lunch stop to be confronted with a sea of mud and slime, your only company rotting cycle and pram frames, old tyres and the pleasant tinkling sound of the local sewer discharging into the mud. The Wye, the Solway Firth, and various tidal stretches of our large industrial rivers, such as the Thames, Tees, Mersey, Tyne and many others, exhibit similar unpleasant characteristics at low tide. In such a situation you have few choices! Until the tide rises you can either read a book or you

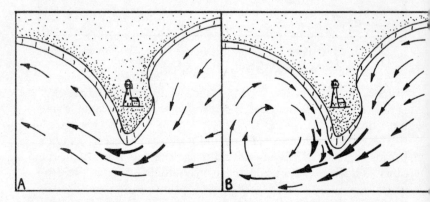

Figure 79. Water behaviour off a headland. Although the tidal stream is running around the headland at a fast speed in A, it should be possible to negotiate the point. But if the opportunity is missed and the tidal stream runs at its maximum, it could produce a fast and dangerous back eddy as in B, which when it meets the main tide race could produce large eddies and whirlpools.

can set off dragging your canoe behind you, probing the mud in front with your paddle. If the mud gets too deep you would be well advised to sit on your canoe grasping your paddle firmly and jerk and kick your way to the nearest solid landing. Setting off to 'squelch' and wade over a large expanse of mud, the depth of which varies from a few inches to an unknown number of feet, could at best be unpleasant and at worst prove fatal. So take care and work out your landing times correctly.

As the tidal streams travel around our coast, white-water conditions, sometimes of quite gigantic proportions, can be formed. A headland jutting out into a fast-moving tidal stream can cause the water to accelerate off its end, forming a *tide race* (Figure 79), which may extend for some considerable distance. Water rushing through narrows may produce roughly the same sort of water turbulence (Figure 80). Headlands usually have underwater shallows extending well out to sea. Water rushing over these underwater shelves produces what is called an *overfall* (Figure 81), the water falling and tumbling over itself and producing steep and sometimes breaking waves, very close together. In some places the same effect can be seen when fast tidal water passes over slower-moving deep water going in either the same direction or the opposite one, creating what might be called a false bottom and producing a large standing wave going nowhere like something out of a canoe slalomist's nightmare. One such wave seen off the west coast of Scotland by several independent, reliable witnesses has been estimated to be 8 to 12 ft. high. The chart marking in this area shows the water to be about 400 ft. deep.

Where two tidal streams or races move at different speeds, the meeting of these two bodies of water produces a *tide rip*. Off surfing beaches, rips are produced in a different manner (see Chapter 4).

Do not confuse tidal streams with currents which are in fact thermal changes in the water. A good example is the Gulf Stream, which is warm and travels to the British Isles from the Gulf of Mexico at about 3 m.p.h. If it wasn't for this warm current our waters would be frozen over every winter and we really would be emulating the Eskimos in more ways than one.

One final word! The sea-going canoeist *must* make the tidal streams work for him and not against him. Always necessary in the

Figure 80. Tidal streams around islands. Note the build-up of water at the upstream end of the islands accelerating into a *race*, where the fast water hits the slower main tidal stream, which is itself starting to move faster because of the constrictive effect of the islands. The increased tidal speed will form an overfall as the flowing water reaches the point where the depth starts to fall away again after the shallows around the islands.

days of sail,* this still applies to yachts, and how much more so must it be necessary for the canoeist who propels his kayak either with or against the wind and sea by the strength of his arm and nothing more. He is lucky in that his canoe draws only a few inches of water and he can halt his progress towards rocks infinitely quicker than a yacht on the same path. A path extremely close inshore or around headlands is no problem to him, and using small back eddy streams in small bays means that he can, even at an adverse state of the tide, get from the water some help which is forever denied to larger craft.

Old sailing ship maxim: 'Water goes off all promontories and into all bights'.

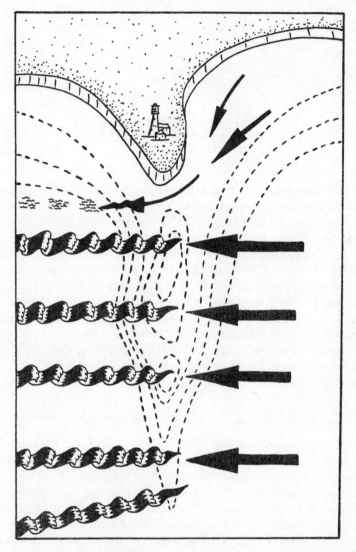

Figure 81. A typical overfall. The rough water associated with this can extend 3 or 4 miles out to sea. The safe passage for a canoeist would be close into the headland unless there is heavy surf, in which case he must paddle just outside the surf line. However, the canoeist must not forget the rough water caused by the race (Figure 80) off the headland, and unless he likes wild conditions, he may have to wait till the tide eases. Overfalls provide good training areas for advanced sea work.

8
Navigation

The term 'navigation' may sound rather grand when talking about canoeing since the equipment on the deck of a sea canoeist's boat hardly turns the deck into a chart table. Yet quite advanced trips and expeditions are undertaken by canoeists.

As basic equipment for planning a trip, the sea canoeist needs charts of the area, Ordnance Survey maps, two rulers and a set of dividers or pencil compasses. Parallel rules are handy but not essential, as is a Sestral navigator. This is just a 360° protractor with a transparent plastic arm which swings round from the centre. It can be homemade quite cheaply and might prove a help in laying off a course. An orienteering compass is also handy. A chinagraph pencil is useful for writing on a waterproof-covered chart if the surface is glassy.

COMPASS

My first compass came out of a 3d lucky bag. It lay in the bottom, next to a whistle-whizzer, a plastic footballer and a 'Move-it-and-the-eyes-wink' coloured picture of Tom and Jerry. I set this tin and cardboard navigational wonder in clear moulding plastic to make it waterproof, then drilled a hole at one end for the string. Many a man has navigated farther with much less. However, a compass is hardly the thing to economise on so get the best you can.

CHARTS

Charts are really the picture story books of the sea. Looking at one

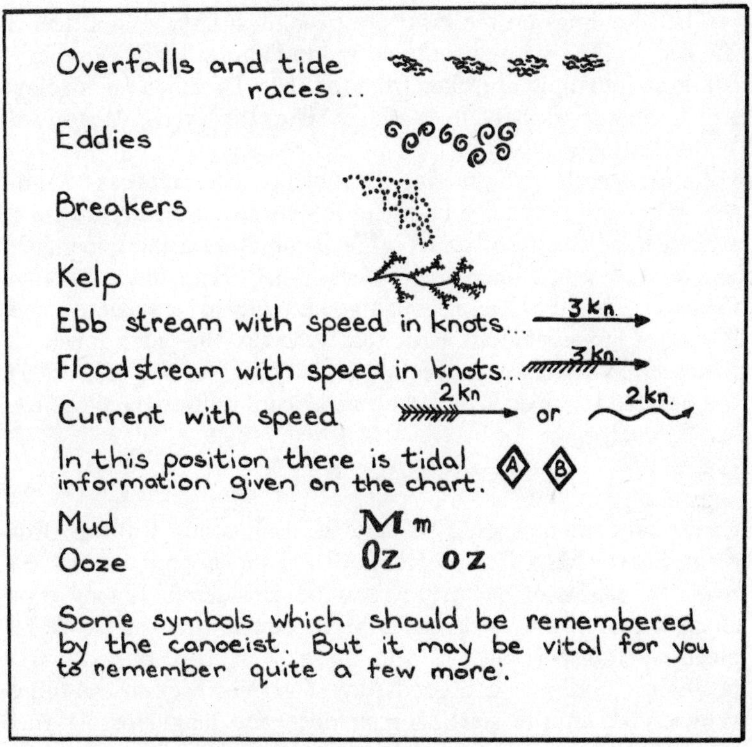

Figure 82. Important chart symbols.

should open up a wonderland of information to you. What is the direction and speed of the tidal stream? What is on the sea bottom—sand or mud? If I make bivouac will there be a spring of fresh water? Will there be overfalls or races to fight against? All these questions should be answered when you look at your chart.

These charts, printed by HM Stationery Office, contain a wealth of information for those who know how to read them. Trying to remember the many abbreviations and symbols on them is an almost impossible job, so it is advisable to buy chart 5011 or to get a copy of *Reed's Nautical Almanac*. Certain symbols should be memorised (Figure 82). After all, when out at sea, the canoeist cannot have a copy of Reed's readily to hand to thumb through at will. He has only his experience and memory to serve him.

The soundings on the chart are marked in fathoms and feet if the depth is less than 11 fathoms and in fathoms only, if deeper.* All these soundings are taken from the chart Datum, a mark below which the tide seldom falls, which is below the level of Mean Low Water Springs.

An ideal protective covering for the chart is Chartseel or Saunseel. Although polythene bags and folders are not really the best, at least the chart is still in its original condition if the water does not get in, whereas once a self-adhesive has been stuck on, it's on for good. Clear Fablon, although good, tends to be reflective and is almost impossible to write on, whereas the matt finish of Saunseel or Chartseel makes a good writing surface. The chart can be fixed to the deck by strong shock cord or it can be taped on.

OS MAPS

Canoe expeditions should be done in conjunction with an Ordnance Survey Map. Camp sites have to be thought out and nearest roads for points of departure must be considered. If long trips along the coast are to be undertaken, careful thought has to be given to transport. When you finish your trip, a previously positioned mini-bus is a good way of getting back to the other vehicles left at the start. I remember one long crossing that meant somebody driving well over 100 miles to position the transport at the other side of the firth.

Weather conditions change for the worse very quickly and a landing spot which permitted a seal landing or a difficult one onto rocks may on the following day prove impossible. This will mean a long portage to find sheltered water again. The Ordnance Survey map will help you find the easiest route. While on the subject of escape routes on land, OS maps give Post Office telephones, AA and RAC boxes, youth hostels, public houses (the Englishman's escape for many years), railway stations and churches. After all, you never know just how bad your luck can turn out. I was once glad of a church to provide shelter for someone in an exposure bag while I waited for assistance from the mainland.

*1 fathom is 6 ft. 1 knot is 1 sea mile per hour. 1 sea mile is approx. 2,020 yd.

DEAD RECKONING

If a canoeist knows the course he paddles and the distance he has travelled, he can use this information to pinpoint his position by what is called dead reckoning. Did I say pinpoint? If the sea were like a lake with no wind or currents, navigation at sea would be rather like fell walking. However, conditions are never quite like that. It is extremely difficult for a canoeist to guess at his speed with tides running and winds blowing. His course, even with a compass, will hardly prove consistent because of the gyrations of his canoe. As in all things, however, practice makes perfect, or should I say *almost* perfect. After settling down to a steady speed over a fixed distance, using a good watch and with some trial and error, the canoeist can learn to work out his average speed under all sorts of varying conditions. He can then calculate the distance he should travel in a fixed time, and this will help him find his position.

CROSS BEARINGS

With your chart in front of you, it is easy to take a cross bearing from two fixed objects on the land. Choose two objects so that after you have taken a bearing on them, the lines drawn from them on your chart are almost at right angles. The point of intersection should indicate your position on the chart.

If you are sitting in your canoe and about to set the course with your compass from a bearing taken from a chart previously, remember that the compass you carry points to magnetic north, *not* true north. If, therefore, your bearing was taken from grid— i.e. from an Ordnance Survey map or the outer ring of the chart compass rose—do not forget to *add* the magnetic variation. This varies between 15 and 9½ degrees, depending where you are in Britain, and is printed on the rose of a chart.

REMEMBER: MAGNETIC TO GRID — *SUBTRACT*
(In the British Isles)
            GRID TO MAGNETIC — *ADD*

If your front pocket is full of car keys, carabiners, a metal torch, a camera and exposure meter and a load of other ironmongery,

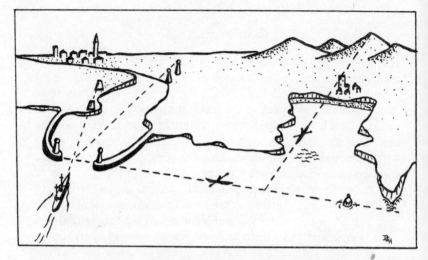

Figure 83. Transits. The canoeist could look backwards and keep the pier lights in line but will more likely line up the buoy and the headland and keep them in transit. He will see immediately any drift caused by an offshore wind. When he sees the church tower in line with the hilltop, he knows it is time to change direction. Keeping them in transit will enable him safely to avoid the broken water over the reef at the entrance to the bay. The ship is using transit towers to guide it between the piers. When the transit beacons are lined up, this tells the ship's captain to change direction towards them. He then uses these to keep him on course up the centre of the channel.

don't wonder why your compass has taken you to Cap Gris Nez when in fact you set out for the end of Brighton Pier.*

TRANSIT BEARINGS

The system of transits is the oldest navigational aid in the world. Ever since men first ventured from land, sailors have set up two posts on a beach so that when they were kept in line the sea-going craft could keep clear of unknown dangers. Any chart or indeed

---

*For a good laugh, place your transistor radio near your compass. Watch what happens and be warned.

OS map will provide an enormous number of ready-to-use transits, such as colliery tower in line with pier, a wireless mast in line with a buoy, one piece of land just jutting out in front of another, or two headlands kept in line. All examples provide either a leading line for the canoeist to keep on, or a position line on a chart, more accurate than a bearing taken by a compass.

The sea canoeist will gain other benefits from the persistent use of transits. Once he is transit minded he will instinctively be aware of how the tidal stream or the wind is setting his canoe, even when he is some distance offshore, without taking any bearing at all. Briefly, the canoeist will develop 'feeling' for his position.

A bearing taken by transit is an ideal way of pinpointing (I mean it) wrecks for skin diving at a later date (if you are that way inclined). You will find the exact place every time by this method, something that cannot be said about taking cross bearings with a compass.

CORRECTING COURSE

It is very easy to be carried away at sea. You can be duped into thinking that the direction you aim for is the direction you go in: far from it.

Here is what happens. In Figure 84 you set off from the coastguard C aiming for the lighthouse L. It is 4 miles away and you are paddling at a steady 4 m.p.h. Suddenly, a curtain of fog blots out the island. Your compass tells you to keep on aiming towards L. The fact you have overlooked is that tidal flow is from right to left at 3 m.p.h. Result: at the end of the hour you will finish up 3 miles to the left of the island. Even if the fog providentially clears to let you see where you are, you will still have another $1\frac{1}{2}$ hours' paddle to beat up against the tide to reach the island.

The solution is to correct your direction of travel, and here is how to do it:

1. You know how fast you can paddle (well, find out then) and in what direction you actually want to travel.
2. You can estimate how much tidal flow there is and in what direction.
3. You can draw (a) and (b) as two sides of a triangle, each side representing direction and speed (shown by length).

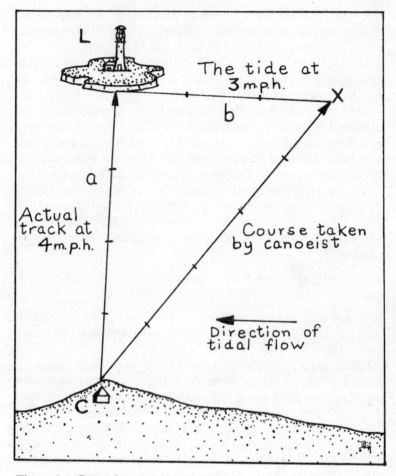

Figure 84. Correcting course.

4. The third side shows you the direction (and incidentally that
    you need 5 m.p.h. to do the distance inside the hour).

    The course bearings are best written next to your cockpit or on
the chart where you can see them. Paddle on the course for an
hour at a constant paddling speed and you should arrive at your
pre-calculated position.

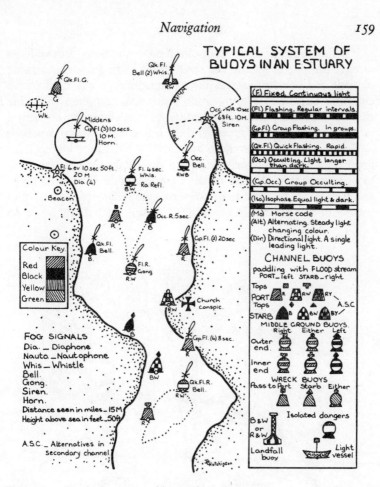

Figure 85. Typical system of buoys in an estuary.

BUOYAGE AND ESTUARIES

Figure 85 shows a typical arrangement of buoys in an estuary. The sea canoeist should know something about these buoys. In dense fog, for instance, you paddle into a large black-coloured buoy with the number 2 written on it. After you paddle a little farther another black conical buoy looms up, this time with a large number 1 on it. Please do not keep on looking for number 0.

It is forbidden to tie up to or climb on to any buoy. In the Tyne estuary the fine is £5 and the river police seem quite enthusiastic in their enforcement of this law. I remember a coaching friend climbing out on to a buoy some years ago, complete with ciné camera. The buoy heaved and rolled quite alarmingly, he went a rather sinister shade of green, and the film-making was postponed.

Take great care in estuaries and tidal rivers. Large vessels have great difficulty in manoeuvring even if they do see you, which is most improbable. Beware of the upstream side of moored ships and barges. Once swept in between two moored ships you will find they tend to squeeze against buffers, closing from about 18 in. to

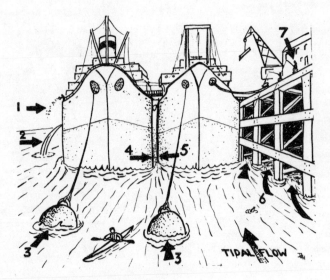

Figure 86. Some danger spots in busy tidal waters.
1.   Crew member finds convenient rubbish tip.
2.   Some of the water gushing from holes in the sides of ships may have ghastly origins.
3.   The upstream side of mooring buoys could cause a capsize.
4, 5. Two ships slowly squeezing together against buffers—a place of *extreme danger*.
6.   To capsize in here could be quite horrific.
7.   Beware of anglers and their lines.

6 in. Your canoe won't stop them and neither will you (Figure 86). You can always tell which way the tide is setting by watching the behaviour of the water around the mooring buoys. It is unwise to practise rolling in estuaries and tidal rivers, but if you feel you must, wear a nose clip, keep your mouth shut and treat yourself afterwards to an antiseptic gargle.

It is well to know the signals a ship will give when it alters course, so that you can take evasive action if necessary:

1 short blast on the hooter means it is going to starboard.

2 short blasts on the hooter means it is going to port.

If you are paddling round the stern of a boat and it gives 3 sharp blasts, get out of the way: it is going to go astern.

In fog, if a vessel is moving, it will give a long blast every 2 minutes, but if it has stopped and is going to sit it out, you will hear 1 blast, then a 1-second gap, another blast, then a space of 2 minutes, then a repetition of the signal again.

ESCAPE ROUTES

These should be thought of well in advance so that if conditions become unfavourable and things in general get a little tense, the leader can take his group out of danger into safety. Figure 87 shows a typical expedition. Oban is the base, the camp site having been found by an OS map. The plan is to paddle down the western exposed sides of the islands of Kerrara, Luing, Scarba and part of Jura.

Any gale from the west will produce extreme paddling conditions, but as can be seen, there are ways back to base which will give reasonable shelter. The routes must be worked out from a chart. If your escape route lies between two islands and the tidal stream is against you, it may be impossible to get into the sheltered water. In such a case you land in the best place you can.

SPECIAL CHALLENGES

Fog

When I first started sea canoeing, very few people ventured out of sight of land. The outlook of most canoeists was very similar to that of sailors prior to the fifteenth century: it wasn't safe and if

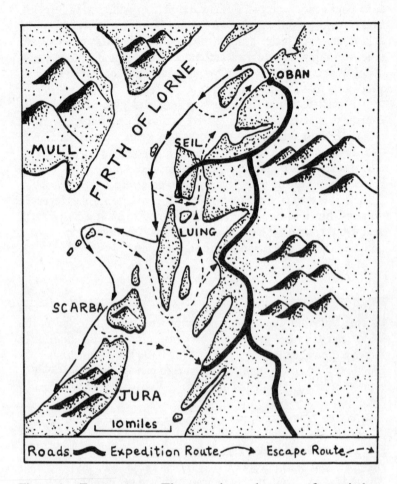

Figure 87. Escape routes. The map shows the route of a typical sea expedition with Oban as the base for transport and main tents. All the escape routes therefore lead either back to base, via the shelter of the islands, or to the nearest road, from which someone will have to walk or hitch-hike to base. Some expeditions offer a variety of escape routes by both land and sea. Some, however, offer none.

the fog was dense the last thing you wanted was to vanish seawards into it. If by some mischance one of those dense summer pea-soup fogs came down, it was out with the compass and grope your way back to the beach.

Be cautious by all means, but don't deprive yourself of some very interesting experiences by never attempting a trip in the fog.

Fog may be present before a trip starts or it can arrive like huge banks of moving steam whilst you are out at sea. It makes no noise as it creeps and envelops everything in its path. Fog is caused when warm air blows off the land over a cool sea and cools the surface air down to its dew point. A clear sky will help the heat to radiate from the earth, and you will see that a slight breeze is needed to carry this warm air.

In really dense fog everything appears and sounds quite different from usual. Buoys and ships take on strange shapes. One minute dogs can be heard barking miles away and the next moment your companion's voice sounds muffled only a few yards away. You lose all sense of direction and after awhile may even doubt your compass. Sometimes the sun seems to give a nice warm glow and the blue sky can be seen when you look up. The fog bank is not very high, and you may even paddle out of it. At other times it seems dark and black even at midday and there is no warm glow. This fog is high, cutting out the sun's bright glare.

If you would like to try a paddle in bad visibility, take your compass and go out a little way offshore into the fog. Don't try this in a harbour at first in case you wander into a shipping lane and get run down. Go off the beach, but not in big surf. Paddle about for 10 minutes or so and then find your way back to the beach. This will give you confidence in your compass. Then go out for about half an hour and wander around just for the thrill of it, knowing you can get back in again when you want to. Go out on a clear day and take some bearings off buoys and markers; then on the next foggy day paddle out and try to locate them. You will soon see how difficult this little exercise can be.

In fog, each member must carry a compass. The chances of getting separated from your group are very great, so you may find that you can actually use the whistle that has been bleached in the sun on its rotting cord on your lifejacket all these years. I often carry a trumpet type of fog horn manufactured by the Acme firm that makes the whistles. Some hand-held fog horns are driven by a can of compressed air. However, everybody will want to play with it so that by the time you need it, instead of a strident hoot there will only be a prolonged and rather embarrassing hiss. In dense fog don't forget you cannot see anything and—what is probably more important—nobody can see you and you will not show up on a ship's radar.

Fog can make the surface of the sea very deceiving. I once set off for an island in fog with the sea like glass and no wind. I was familiar with the water and the distance involved was only a couple of miles, but after I had paddled the time it normally takes to get there, no island loomed up. It appeared it had either sunk or been towed away. I sat and wondered where I had gone wrong. Well, there is a good rule in fog: if you can't see, listen. So I strained my ears and could just hear something to the north, a rather peculiar sound I could not place. I headed towards it and soon the sky was filled with screaming, diving, swooping sea-birds round the cliffs of an island. It was obvious where I had gone wrong. Although the water was calm and smooth, the tidal stream was running very fast. This was obvious, however, only when I looked at the water in relation to the island it was rushing past. Out in the fog the water had appeared quite still, giving no hint that we were being swept farther and farther away from our destination.

Remember then: land has a sound. It may be a train, dogs barking, the sound of birds or a combination of many things. So use your ears and listen carefully for, and be able to identify, the distinctive sounds of land.

The only way to locate something lost in fog—an island, a buoy, anything—is to use your compass and paddle a square. Paddle about 30 strokes for each side and then gradually increase the size of the box, sticking rigidly to compass bearings but of course remembering the drift.

Really thick fog does not usually arrive without warning. There are some ways of being able to predict it. First of all, was there fog yesterday or the day before? If the answer is yes and the general weather conditions have not changed, the chance is there may well be fog today.

Look at the surface of the sea. Is it hazy and is the horizon hazy and indistinct? Is the air blowing off the land and across the cool sea? All these are sure indications of fog, and it will be as well during the summer to pay attention to such tell-tale signs and *to carry a compass for even the shortest trip offshore.*

Night Canoeing

The first time most people find out what it is like to canoe at night is usually on a late return from a day's paddle. Whatever the reason, you now find yourself in a completely different situation, so you may as well enjoy it. Paddling at night is an exciting and interesting experience, and canoeing by the light of the moon can be almost like paddling on a moonbeam.

Lights may be confusing as to their number and location. It is quite easy to misinterpret the headlights of a car as it passes over the brow of a hill near the shore line. Don't forget that from seawards, flashing buoys are seen against a backcloth of shimmering shore lights and can easily be missed. Lighthouses always seem

Figure 88. Navigation lights.

to look nearer at night than they really are. Sometimes you may see as many as five or six all winking and flashing different colours. The most common type of light you will come across on your paddles is group flashing (Gp. Fl. on your chart) from a lighthouse, which is a set number of flashes repeated at a fixed interval. You cannot get an accurate bearing by using these flashes, but lighthouses often have different coloured segments and in such cases you can get a bearing line as you pass from, say, the green segment to the red, since the division between the colours is shown on all admiralty charts. At night when vessels are stationary, their lights are usually very bright. Fishing boats may have their decks floodlit. I well remember coming upon a fishing boat at about 2 a.m. out of the blackness into the illuminated area surrounding the boat and being greeted with a certain amount of alarm by the white-faced man working on the deck.

All ships—all except you, that is—must show navigation lights: white masthead lights, with the one on the front mast lower than that on the rear mast, and a red light on the port side and a green light on the starboard side. Remember that from your low position on the water, the masthead lights may look almost level. Figure 88 shows some interesting combinations.

A man 40 feet or more up on the bridge of a ship has a completely different view of lights and of traffic on the water from that of a canoeist. He cannot see you at all; you are completely invisible. By the time someone in the wheelhouse has made up his mind that he has actually seen your little new waterproof torch and has then found some deck officer to make sure through his steamed-up glasses that it *was* a light, you are still in trouble, because he is travelling at 10 to 20 knots and is thus not likely to be able to slow down quickly. I know that when I must cross a shipping channel in the dark, I sit looking and listening for some time and then I cross at a speed that would do credit to a rather highly strung greyhound. If necessary, white or green hand flares can be fired to draw a boat's attention to your position. (Don't set off a blue one, or you will get the local pilot coming out to you, and will he be pleased!)

Probably the most important piece of equipment you will need and use, apart from what you normally carry, is a caver's headlamp or, failing this, a waterproof torch taped to your helmet. You will need this light for studying the chart and livening up the some-times feeble glow of your luminous compass. However, bear in mind that some caver's lamps are not as waterproof as one would wish. You will also want another waterproof torch handy on the foredeck (fastened to the canoe by a cord), which will have many uses, but *not* for warning ships of any size of your presence.

As a night navigator you will, of course, make a note of the specific lights you will encounter before setting out on a trip. For an example of what you might expect, see Figure 85, 'Typical system of buoys in an estuary'.

Paddling at night should be tried only after you are a very com-petent daylight paddler. The leader must know his group and keep it small. Remember that it is one thing paddling through rough water when you can see what your paddle is going into or the speed at which the water is moving, and it is another thing entirely when you can hardly see anything.

9

Arctic Origins
of the Sea Canoe

Some of the horrors that float about on our coastal waters under the name of sea canoes bear little or no resemblance to the designs developed over many hundreds of years by the indigenous inhabitants of the Arctic. The genuine sea canoe of the Arctic was evolved by adapting a particular type of canoe to specific needs and conditions. Throughout its history it has been essentially a completely seaworthy boat in order to fulfil its primary function of being a hunter's boat.

The Eskimo has always had a constant fight for survival against what would seem overwhelming difficulties—the long dark winter, the eternal cold, and the never-ending search for food. The only element which can provide subsistence is the sea. It is here that the Eskimo gets most of his food, from fish or from sea mammals such as the seal, walrus, sea otter and the whale. From these animals he also gets oil for his lamps and sinews and baleen for sewing skins and furs. The ivory and bones from these animals, as well as from his own dogs, can be made into weapons, tools, domestic implements and ornaments. The only other raw material available is driftwood, which floats in large quantities down rivers like the Yukon and Mackenzie and is then spread around the seas of the Arctic along the northern shores of Russia and the coasts of Greenland. But the right type of driftwood is rare and the scarcity of wood necessitates the retrieval of harpoon shafts while hunting and makes the kayak a highly prized piece of equipment, handed down from father to son.

The Eskimo used to hunt the whale in an open boat about 30 ft. long and 6 ft. wide with a flat bottom. It was propelled by women and was named the umiak (the Russian word is baydara) or 'woman's boat'. Hunting the walrus and seal required a different type of boat altogether from the umiak, so the Eskimo developed what is probably the most famous single-handed craft in the world. For elegance, grace and austere beauty, it has never been surpassed by any other type of solo canoe. Since it also boasts speed, silence and seaworthiness, this is a true kayak or 'hunter's boat'.

When the Eskimo built a kayak, the frame was constructed first. Two long planks from 2 to 7 in. wide were used as gunwales, which were secured fore and aft in a position to take the bow and stern posts. The gunwales were supported by cross members or deck beams. Lashed on top of these with seal thong was a lath which ran down the centre of the deck. Rib frames of bent wood were mortised into the gunwale planks. The kayak was then turned on to its deck. A longitudinal lath was lashed to the bottom in the centre and an even number of laths, usually either 4 or 6, secured at either side. Any slight gaps between the bent frames and the laths could be packed out by thick pieces of hide to stop the frames distorting (Figure 98). The frame was then covered tightly with seal-skin from which all the hair had been plucked. A small man-hole was left in the deck. This was fitted with a wooden hoop coaming through which the skin was tightly stretched and tacked over with bone or ivory pins. As the skin shrank, it drew the coaming even tighter to the deck. When finished the kayak had to be light enough to be carried by the paddler either over his shoulder with his arm inside the manhole or, in the case of some Greenland kayaks, on his head with the cockpit coaming resting against his forehead. A walk from one bay to the next might save many miles of paddling, or make the difference between launching on a lee or weather shore.

In winter the man wore a hairless seal-skin jacket with a hood. This was the anorak or 'full smock'. The bottom hem of this could be pulled over the cockpit coaming and lashed tightly round the hoop with a long piece of thong. Two strips of narrow bone beading 6 or 7 in. long and about $\frac{1}{4}$ in. wide were fixed by pins to the top edge of the coaming at the back. The two other pieces were fixed parallel to these but lower down (Figure 98). This arrangement formed a locating channel for the thong when it was wrapped around. Although the anorak was secured in this way only at the rear of the cockpit, it is doubtful whether the hunter would be able to wrench the jacket free in an emergency, so that a roll or an assisted rescue would be his only means of salvation.

In southern Alaska and the Aleutian Islands the hunter would wear a longer garment made from horizontal strips of seal-gut,* called the kamleika (originally this Russian word meant 'fur coat'). The 'half-frock', another garment worn by the hunter, was more like our spray cover. It was a short skirt of seal-skin tied round the cockpit rim to keep out the water and also tied under the armpits if necessary.

Kayaks from the far north of Greenland and certain parts of Hudson Bay have larger cockpits which are left unsealed** (Figure 89). Hunting the walrus can be very dangerous and if the prey turns and comes into the attack, the hunter can leave his kayak much more quickly if he is not fastened by thongs to the cockpit coaming. If the walrus slashes huge rents in the skin of his own boat, he can always seek safety on the deck of a companion's boat, thus saving himself from the wrath of the walrus, the bitter cold of the water, or death by drowning. It is almost unheard of for an Eskimo to swim.

Kayaks vary in pattern and shape, each having its own distinctive sea-going qualities and style. Each kayak is also tailored to the body measurements of the individual paddler and is worn like a garment rather than just 'sat in' like a rowing boat. To get into the boat the man first sits on the back deck, puts both feet up inside the canoe and wriggles until he is firmly in the manhole. His back is jammed against one of the cross beams protruding into the cockpit space. This means that any strain is taken on the wooden strut rather than by the wooden hoop. The hunter uses one of the curved hull frames as a footrest, and the kayak becomes rather like an extension of the man's body, responding to his every move.

Although methods of measuring may differ slightly, the system is basically the same. For instance the King Islander makes his canoe gunwales $2\frac{1}{2}$ arm spans long. The stem piece which has a

---

*Seal-gut was 3 in. in diameter and when opened out it provided a strip 6 in. wide. Walrus-gut was even wider.

**R. Frank, *Frozen Frontier, The Story of the Arctic*, George G. Harrap, 1964.

Figure 89. North Greenland/Hudson Bay kayak. This kayak is rather ugly when compared with other Greenland kayaks. The wide deck is flat except for the sheer up to the large round cockpit. Note the high wooden coaming. The man appears to sit quite loosely and slumped back. The paddle, drawn to scale, is long by Eskimo standards. In the photo which inspired this drawing, what appeared to be a large full dustbin stood on the deck just forward of the cockpit; this may give some indication of the stability of this particular kayak.

notch at the top to locate the gunwales is the distance from the elbow to the finger tips (a cubit). The two middle thwarts are as long as the outstretched arm including the fingers. This makes the width about 25 in., but the flared sides bring the waterline beam down to about 18 in.

The King Islander had to face not only the very stormy waters of the Bering Sea but also a launching problem. His walrus-gut parka* was secured tightly round the cockpit coaming and he and his boat were then picked up by 4 men and thrown into the sea. His kayak therefore had to be very strong, so that just any wood was not good enough. The gunwales had to be straight-grained and matched. For the 10 thwarts, natural curved pieces of wood were used and the 25 to 30 rib frames were split from birch logs and bent by steaming. The willow cockpit hoop was an integral part of the framework. Compare this robust construction with that of the Nunamiut kayak.

*From the Russian word for shirt. The Eskimo word is ee-maln-ee-tik.

The Nunamiuts, members of an inland tribe, lived by hunting the caribou in a kayak about 20 ft. long. The gunwales were 2 spruce strips bound together at the ends by rawhide thongs. The U shaped ribs were green willow shoots the thickness of a man's thumb, bent and then mortised into the gunwales to form the hull. The 5 or 7 longitudinal laths were strips of birch or spruce which did not extend completely to the stern or stem, where slender deck beams of willows were fixed, much less curved than the other beams. Even though this kayak was nowhere near so robust as its coastal cousin, it had violent usage.

Figure 90. Nunivak Island kayak. This and the King Island kayak are regarded as the safest and most seaworthy of all Eskimo kayaks. Paddler and passenger sit back to back in the same cockpit. One can only wonder what private arrangements are made between the two men in the event of a capsize.

This kayak could be pushed or pulled across the snow, riding on its own small sledge which was carried on the back deck when the kayak was being used in the usual way. This accounts for the hand grips at the bow and stern.* The hole in the bow was also a convenient resting place for the end of the harpoon when it was secured on the foredeck, and it has been suggested that the hole would reduce the effect of a beam wind catching the bow. Because the cockpit was so large, the hunter could leap in and out quickly if the need arose. The high deck was designed to give plenty of room inside so that when used for hunting, large bulky quantities of meat could be carried. It had to be steeply pitched to reduce the action of the wind and provide a surface which would throw off the heavy seas.

*Adney and Chappell, *The Bark Canoes and Skin Boats of North America,* Smithsonian Institute.

The migrating herds of caribou were frightened into making river crossings at places previously chosen by the Eskimos. The women would creep up and frighten the herd towards the river. Piles of stones called inukshuks, which at a distance looked like groups of people (Figure 91), were used to divert the terrified animals to the chosen spot. Once in the water the herd was at the mercy of the kayak men who paddled amongst them, stabbing them with a spear high in the rib cage to one side of the backbone, piercing the heart or lungs. The thrust and withdrawal had to be quick, or the animal would thrash about and the man could be overturned and pitched in the icy water among the surging animals.

Some tribes such as the Aivilingmiuts used a heavy kayak for walrus and seal hunting and a lighter one for lake work and caribou hunting. But the Caribou Eskimos used a kayak similar to the one illustrated in Figure 96 for both purposes. If they were going to hunt sea mammals the kayak frame was covered with seal-skin, whereas if caribou were to be the victims then the same frame was covered with caribou skin. The Itiumiut Eskimos also had different kayaks for inland and sea work, and it is obvious that the Eskimo came to the same conclusion as that arrived at by so many modern paddlers—that there is no such thing as a general purpose boat for both river and sea.

A Greenland kayak equipped for hunting seals had a framework platform or tray called the kayak stand on the foredeck to carry a long coiled line (Figure 92). One end of the line was secured to the detachable head of the hunter's harpoon and the other end led under his arm to the back deck and was fixed to a large seal-skin float which itself was attached to the rear deck in a quick-release manner. Lying on the foredeck next to the harpoon might be a lance while underneath the kayak stand, safe in its bag, would be a rifle.

Hidden behind a white camouflage shield mounted on the fore-deck, the hunter would look for the seals. As soon as he saw his prey the hunter would paddle into range and, quickly shipping his paddle, withdraw the gun and fire. Then, gun away, he would paddle swiftly within harpoon range. The paddle would be pushed under the deck thong again and the harpoon hurled accurately and forcibly with the assistance of the throwing stick. During the time the kayak was running free with no paddle, it might have been held on course by means of a detachable skeg. As soon as the

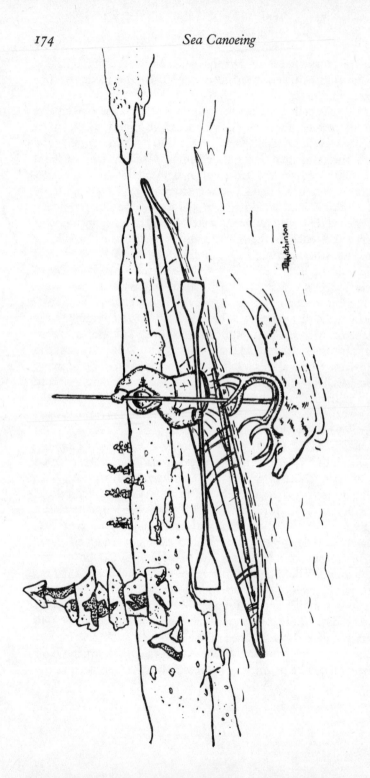

Figure 91. The death of a caribou. Note the inukshuks in the background and the way the hunter keeps hold of his paddle rather than pushing it under the deck thongs as he would do if he were harpooning a seal.

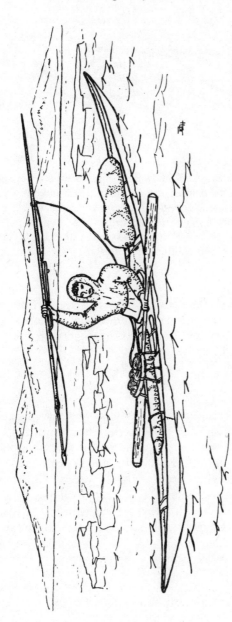

Figure 92. Seal-hunting Eskimo.

length 9ft.

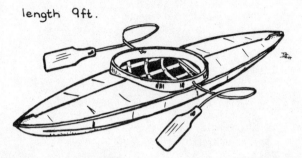

Figure 93. Koryak kayak (Kamchatka). The Koryaks were a gentle people. There was no comparison between them and the daring sea canoeists of the Aleutian Islands. This kayak, which would probably manoeuvre rather like a modern baths canoe, was used on the sea, but only on calm water. Note the thwart that acts as a back support. The small wooden hand paddles are fastened to the cockpit coaming by seal thongs.

prey was harpooned, the flotation bag was released from the rear deck. Thus if the prey was killed immediately it would not sink, or if it was only wounded and dived, it would then tire with the drag of the inflated bag.

The Baffinland kayak

This kayak from Baffin Bay (Figure 95) looks rather ungainly with its huge thick bow and flat squat stern. The cockpit slopes down towards the flat back deck and is horseshoe shaped. Apart from the forefoot at the bow, the boat is virtually flat bottomed. In spite of its rather unwieldy appearance, however, this kayak was reputedly easy to turn, presumably sliding round over the water on its flat bottom. However, its seaworthiness in extreme conditions must be suspect, because of this same flat bottom (see the section on hull shapes in Chapter 1).

The Caribou kayak

This kayak (Figure 96) came from the north-western shores of Hudson Bay. Although the caribou were hunted mainly at river

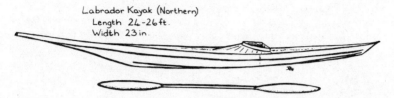

Labrador Kayak (Northern)
Length 24-26ft.
Width 23in.

Figure 94. Labrador kayak (northern). Like the Baffin Bay kayak, this also has a flat bottom and is very stable. It is strongly built, heavy and very seaworthy. The cockpit is horseshoe shape, flat along the back. The superb clipper bow is 5 ft. long. To assist in turning this very long kayak, the pautic or paddle is 10 ft. long.

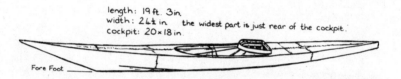

length: 19 ft. 3in.
width: 24½in   the widest part is just rear of the cockpit.
cockpit: 20×18in.

Fore Foot

Figure 95. North Baffinland kayak. It is not rolled by the men who paddle it: in the event of a capsize the hunter would bail out and hope for speedy assistance while hanging onto the upturned boat.

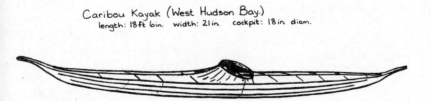

Caribou Kayak (West Hudson Bay.)
length: 18ft 6in.   width: 21in   cockpit: 18in diam.

Figure 96. Caribou kayak (West Hudson Bay).

M

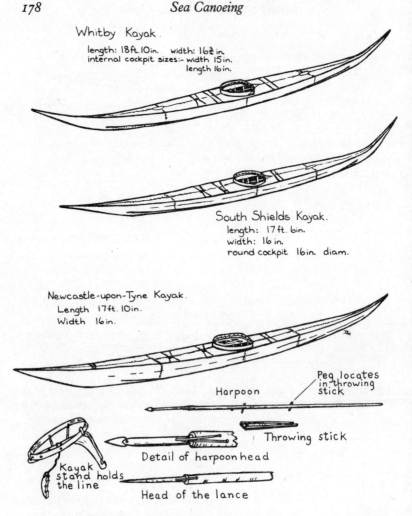

Whitby Kayak.
length: 18 ft. 10 in.   width: 16¾ in.
internal cockpit sizes:- width 15 in.
                    length 16 in.

South Shields Kayak.
length: 17 ft. 6 in.
width: 16 in.
round cockpit 16 in. diam.

Newcastle-upon-Tyne Kayak.
Length 17 ft. 10 in.
Width 16 in.

Peg locates in throwing stick

Harpoon

Throwing stick

Detail of harpoon head

Kayak stand holds the line

Head of the lance

Figure 97. West Greenland kayaks.

crossings, they were also driven into small open-water lakes and
were forced to cross narrow sea fjords.

When viewed in plan and elevation, the Caribou kayak could be
compared quite closely with a modern competition slalom canoe,
as it has a considerable rocker. The only real differences are the
slender willowy bow and stern of the Caribou kayak and its

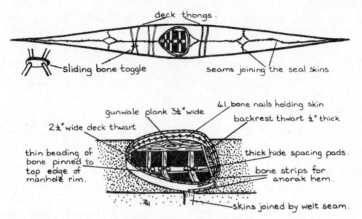

Figure 98. Whitby kayak: plan view and detail of cockpit.

obviously seaworthy cockpit. A group of kayak hunters paddling in amongst a herd of frightened swimming caribou needed a canoe that would turn very quickly and had a strong covering, and a bow that could safely hook into the antlers of an escaping animal and divert it long enough for a companion to close in for the coup de grâce.

Greenland kayaks

Kayaks from this huge, sprawling landmass, specifically the designs from the west coast of Greenland, have influenced modern sporting sea canoes more than any other type of Eskimo kayak. It was difficult to know which particular types would best illustrate the qualities of the West Greenland kayak. After a great deal of examining, measuring and sketching, I chose three which best illustrate not only the superb sea-going qualities but also the subtle local differences in design. I refer to all three kayaks by the names of the museums where they are to be found—South Shields, Whitby and Newcastle (Figure 97).

It will be seen that the kayaks from South Shields and Whitby have extremely high sterns. There were very good reasons for this. When the hunter approached his quarry from down wind, the

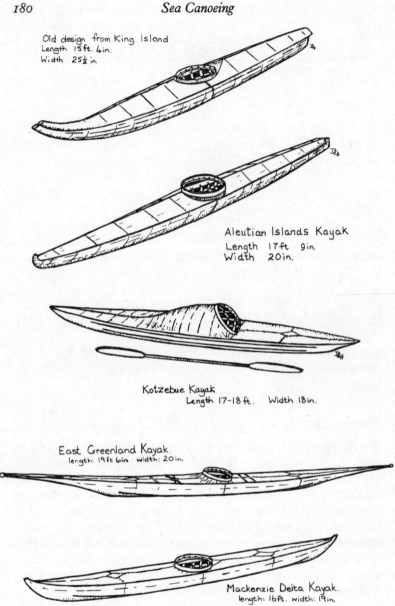

Old design from King Island
Length 15ft. 4in.
Width 25½in.

Aleutian Islands Kayak
Length 17ft 9in.
Width 20in.

Kotzebue Kayak
Length 17-18ft.   Width 18in.

East Greenland Kayak.
length: 19ft 6in   width: 20in.

Mackenzie Delta Kayak.
length: 16ft. width: 19in.

Figure 99. Other Eskimo kayaks.

high stern would act as a kind of rudder. This meant that the kayak would continue to travel forwards, held straight and true, while the hunter, shipping his paddle, could fire his rifle or throw a harpoon. The bow and stern of the Newcastle kayak are less exaggerated and much lower than the other two, but the hull aft of the cockpit is very narrow, rising gently to a low, slim stern.

All three kayaks are rather straight sided and almost flat bottomed. It seems incredible than an adult male even of Eskimo proportions could get into any of the cockpits, since the width of all the hulls is only 16 in. at its widest part and the internal measurements at the cockpit can be as small as 15 in. Leg room is no less of a problem. The South Shields kayak has only 6 in. from the deck thwart in front of the cockpit to the bent frame at the bottom of the hull, into which a man must squeeze his feet, legs and thighs. It is hardly surprising that modern manufacturers when trying to imitate Eskimo designs have had to make considerable modifications to accommodate the European man.

East Greenland kayak

This differs in design from the other Greenland kayaks illustrated (Figure 99). Its length—usually 18 ft. but up to 20 ft.—and its long, low clipper bow and long, low stern makes it a very fast hunting machine, with little for a beam wind to catch. As with all Greenland kayaks, the primary function was to carry a man while he hunted seal in sheltered waters amongst ice flows or fjords. In design it was not really meant for the use to which sporting canoeists now put it. Paddling into a steep head sea in any kind of wind would be a wet, chilling and dangerous business. Because its lines embody speed and slender grace, the design has been used as a basis for some modern kayaks of a similar type. The really roughwater kayaks, however, are those from the Aleutian and Alaskan areas.

The early King Island kayak and the Kotzebue Sound kayak

Both these kayaks are outlandish, perhaps even quaint in appearance, but no less seaworthy because of it. The bow of the early-type King Island kayak (Figure 99) would rise beautifully to short steep seas while the steeply pitched deck would quickly shed heavy water breaking over it. Like the more modern King Island kayak (see Plate 12), it was paddled with a single-bladed paddle except when the double-bladed paddle was used for speed during hunting.

The Kotzebue Sound kayak (Figure 99) with its low freeboard and flat deck would be constantly awash in anything but a reasonably calm sea, although I cannot imagine any water gaining access to the canoe via the manhole. With this tremendous amount of buoyancy amidships coupled with the flat deck, its rolling qualities can only be guessed at. Fast hunting-paddling was done with a double blade.

Kayak from the Aleutian Islands

Any account of Eskimo kayaks would be incomplete without a mention of the baidarkas (the Russian name for kayak) of the Aleutian Islands, which have some of the most dangerous waters in the world. (See figures 99 and 101). To hunt the whale and the sea-otter, the Aleuts used a narrow two-manhole baidarka 21 ft. long by 23 in. wide. It was very shallow and in cross section the bottom was round and therefore very difficult to keep upright.

When hunting the sea-otter the Eskimos formed themselves into groups, from a few pairs to perhaps 100 on the water at one time. The front man in the canoe used a spear while the man in the rear cockpit manoeuvred the canoe with a long double-bladed paddle. The flotilla would move quietly along in a line until someone saw an otter on the surface. He would raise a paddle in the air to warn the others and then paddle to the sea-otter's last position on the surface of the water before its dive,* where the rest of the group would form a large circle around him. As soon as the sea-otter resurfaced, the nearest hunter paddled towards it, giving the animal no time to fill its lungs. This happened time and time again until the duration of the dives got shorter and shorter. The hunters would then close in and the animal could be speared.

If the wind was violent and the air filled with rain and spray, a tired sleepy animal might lie on the top of the kelp beds, its head hidden under the floating seaweed. In such a case the hunters

*Harold McCracken, *Hunters of the Stormy Sea*, Oldbourne, 1957.

Figure 100. Whale hunting from a baidarka.

could stealthily approach close enough to strike out and kill the unsuspecting creature with a wooden club.

Perhaps the greatest conquest of all for the kayak hunter was the killing of a whale. Once these huge mammals were sighted, only the bravest and most experienced hunters with the strongest and heaviest and sharpest of harpoons would dare take to the water. Paddling out amongst the feeding school, the hunters would select the small calves for their attention. To force the harpoon deep enough into the whale for a kill, the men would have to position themselves about 10 to 15 ft. away, and then throw the harpoon with the full force of the throwing stick, aiming for a point just below the huge dorsal fin.* On feeling the pain, the whale would explode into thrashing violence, its flukes waving high above the hunters before crashing down and churning up the water (Figure 100). It would not be unknown to the whale-hunting Eskimos to

*Ibid.

be killed by 'the hand of God', the name given in the Azores to these giant tails that would crash down onto the whaling 'canoas'.* With any luck, however, the baidarka would manoeuvre clear of the injured whale and also of any enraged bull or cow swimming near.

The Aleut might have been hunting the whale to this day had not greedy, vicious men thousands of miles away taken a hand in his destiny and altered his way of life forever. In 1725 Vitus Bering, a Dane, led a Russian expedition of geographic exploration to Siberia and the north Pacific coast. Survivors from this ill-fated venture took sea-otter pelts back to Russia, which excited the Russians so much that they sent other expeditions to obtain more furs. Many of the men who elected to go could see fortunes for themselves on the horizon. They were the human dregs of Siberia, pirates with no moral code or thought for human life. Their code of conduct was ruled by the knowledge that punishment for crimes was non-existent: 'God is high above, and the Czar is far away'.** These were the promyshleniki, the professional hunters. By murder and intimidation, the native Eskimos, the Aleuts, were taken hostage, enslaved and forced to hunt the sea-otter until it almost vanished from the area. The Russians then had to turn their attentions farther afield, as far south as the coast of California. While the promyshleniki travelled in the comparative comfort of large boats called shitikas,*** the Aleuts were forced to paddle their baidarkas over distances which can only be described as appalling. In the summer of 1783 a veritable armada of large boats with scores of accompanying Aleut hunters set off from Unalaska for Prince William Sound, a distance of over 1000 miles across storm-swept open sea. Fear of the knout and the knowledge that their wives and daughters were on board the shitikas kept the Aleuts paddling night and day at about 10 miles

---

*Trevor Housby, *The Hand of God, Whaling in the Azores*, Abelard-Schuman, 1971.

**McCracken, *op.cit.*

***Because of the shortage of materials and tools, the Russians built their boats from roughly shaped timbers fastened together by hide thongs in the absence of nuts, bolts and nails. Thus sewn together (shi-it is Russian 'to sew', hence shitika), some of the early models literally fell to pieces only a few miles from land, drowning the crews.

per hour, unable to stop, sleeping in the kayaks by turns, unable even to relieve themselves properly. Journeys such as these, with fear of stragglers or the sick being shot,* must have been a nightmare and reflect no credit on the colonising Russians of the eighteenth century. It is fortunate that the baidarka with its bifed stem was probably the finest sea kayak in an area of fine kayaks and that the Aleuts were brilliant sea canoeists.

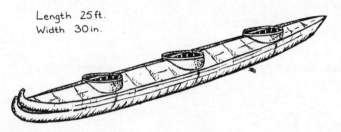

Length 25 ft.
Width 30 in.

Figure 101. Three-manhole baidarka (Southern Alaska and Aleutian Islands).

The three-manhole baidarka (Figure 101) invented by the Russians to carry a passenger or goods was much larger than the two-hole hunter's boat. The single-manhole boat could also be used for seal hunting, while the clumsy family baidarkas could carry dogs, children, furs, wife, meat, nets and all the other luxuries of life. What faith in their husband's canoeing ability these women must have had in order to huddle happily inside the claustrophobic hull. The order of packing and distribution of the cargo (dogs with meat, wife or children?) can only be wondered at.

It is sad to think that many of the kayak and hunting skills described in this chapter are dying out or are already a thing of the past. The whaling carried on by the Aleuts died forever during the 100-year Russian tyranny. The King Islanders no longer live on their rocky island but are now housed on the mainland and display their kayak skills mainly to impress the tourists. The Danish government is doing good work in encouraging the Greenland Eskimos to maintain and preserve their culture and way of life, but even many of their kayaks are now built with canvas and

*McCracken, *op. cit.*

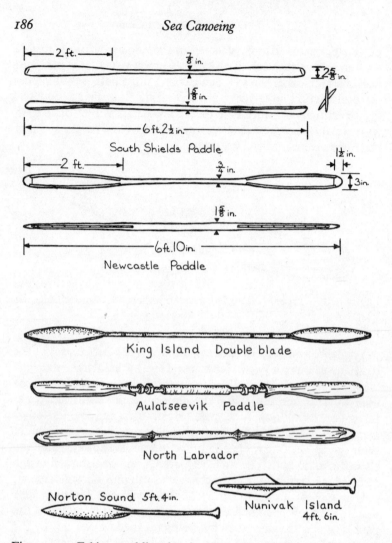

Figure 102. Eskimo paddles showing diversity of styles.

joined with nails. Fortunately, nails don't rust in the cold dry atmosphere. The Eskimo is no longer dependent on his own skills for survival, and the kayak, the hunter's boat, sadly may soon be gone forever. However it is to be hoped that designers will preserve the tradition of the Eskimo kayak even if in glassfibre, and that people will be encouraged to learn to handle what must surely be the most demanding yet the most rewarding boat in the world.

ESKIMO PADDLES

At one time my idea of a typical Eskimo paddle was like the Newcastle paddle in Figure 102, which is from West Greenland. These paddles displayed a high degree of workmanship, with bone beading to stop the sides of the blade chafing and bone ends made from the shoulder-plate of a dog. Although some of the paddle looms from this area were rectangular in cross section, the majority I have seen have been oval, giving a firm, comfortable and positive hand grip. However, Eskimo paddle designs are almost as numerous as the kayak designs themselves.

Quite a number of paddles have some kind of anti-capillary groove or ring. Water constantly running down the loom onto the hands could be more than uncomfortable in freezing temperatures with a wind blowing, even if mittens were sometimes worn. The function of these anti-capillary devices is a little different from that of the one-time popular drip rings, which were used in the older European type of canoe before the adoption of spray covers. The idea behind these rings was to stop water running down the loom, down the arm and then dripping uncomfortably off the elbow, thus entering the large cockpit and then onto the knees and into the boat.

In Figure 102 the North Labrador paddle has shaped pieces to shed the water at the extremities of the loom. It was probably a very satisfactory arrangement. The Aulatseevik paddle seems to be the ultimate in Eskimo paddle comfort.* In a photograph I have seen of this, all the wide sections appeared to be bone sheathing an oval wooden interior. The hands were positioned in the space between the wide centre piece and the first bobbin; next came another drip ring to stop any stray drops of water which may have escaped the efficient looking anti-capillary curve at the beginning of the blade. This Rolls-Royce of paddles was photographed lying across the cockpit of an Eskimo kayak, the interior of which was lined with what appeared to be white polar bear fur. The owner of

*D. Wilkinson, *Land of the Long Day*.

this outfit was obviously a man who valued his creature comforts—
I know the feeling well.

The most distinctive feature of the Labrador paddle is its length
(Figure 94). It is hardly surprising, of course, that a boat of up to
26 ft. should need a large paddle 10 ft. long. An even longer paddle
was used by the Nunamiut tribe, whose kayak has already been
described. In front of the cockpit, a forked piece of willow or alder
tree was used as a pivot for the almost 20-ft.-long paddle, which
was hewn from spruce log.*

Spare paddles were sometimes carried by the hunters, especially
those who used the single- and double-bladed paddles, such as the
Eskimos of Alaska and some of the offshore islands, although I have
never heard of Greenland Eskimos carrying spare paddles.

When the Eskimo gripped a double-bladed paddle, his hands
were positioned about 4 hand-widths apart. This is quite close
compared with modern practice, but anyone who tries to paddle
in freezing conditions and wants to keep his hands dry without
drip rings will find the Eskimo hand position practical. How the
Koryaks (Figure 94) managed with their little hand paddles is not
known to me. I've often wondered if through the years they
developed extra long arms.

The Eskimo never used a feathered blade. Various theories have
been put forward as to why this should be. Some say the blade is so
narrow that the retardation caused by a head wind is hardly
noticeable. The reason may, however, be much simpler: he may
never have thought of it.

While investigating the various kayaks, I was surprised to see,
lying in the cockpit of the South Shields kayak in storage at the
local museum, a paddle which was feathered at 45° for a left-
handed paddler (Figure 102). This may sound strange, considering
the blades are of course flat, but it is extremely difficult to manipu-
late this paddle while trying to paddle right-handed. The loom is
oval and has no twist along its entire length. Only the paddle
blades themselves twist gently along their length, finally setting
themselves at 45° to each other at the end.

---

*Nicholas J. Gubsen, *The Nunamiut Eskimos, Hunters of the Caribou*,
Yale University Press, 1965.

Conclusion

The whole coast of Britain, with its many islands, is suitable for sea canoeing expeditions which can open the door to adventure, thrills, discovery and to many strange and beautiful experiences.

It would take another book to recount the tales I have to tell. There is room here only to make passing reference to a few incidents—the pleasure of observing in all seasons the grey seals of the Farne Islands; the beautiful and eerie night trip around the Farnes when the phosphorescent plankton illuminated our wake with myriads of stars, and hundreds of birds flapped around our heads without uttering a single cry; the extreme tension during the paddle through fog across the Firth of Forth for the Isle of May and the tremendous feeling of elation when we realised our compass work had been accurate; the hilarity of finding that all discussion about pitching our tent to face the sunrise, the sunset or the prevailing wind had been an ironic waste of time, when we lay under the charred, flapping remnants after someone had set fire to it while making the coffee; the incredible satisfaction of overcoming everything the sea could throw at us, the freezing cold, the pounding waves breaking on reefs, the huge Atlantic swell, the lashing fury of a Force 8 gale, and, to add to the confusion, a 7 knot tidal stream cutting across our path as we slogged our way across the Sound of Harris to the coast of North Uist.

Finally, sea canoeing is not just for the young; it is for the young in heart. It is for those adventurous spirits who want to fly with the wild swans instead of languishing safely and dully in the farmyard pond.

Appendix 1

Rather than give a list of tidal constants in times which although accurate are difficult and inconvenient to remember, I have simplified the use of such information by rounding up all the time differences to the nearest 5 minutes, as certainly no canoeist that I know of needs anything more precise than that.

The following is based on H.W. Dover:

East Coast		
Burnham-on-Crouch	+1.05	
Maldon	+1.30	
West Mersea	+1.00	
Brightlingsea	+0.40	
Wivenhoe	+0.50	
Walton-on-Naze	+0.15	
Harwich	+0.25	
Aldeburgh	−0.50	
Lowestoft	−2.00	
Blakeney	−4.45	
Wells	−4.35	
Hunstanton	−5.10	
Wisbech Cut	−5.00	
Kings Lynn	−5.00	
Grimsby	−5.40	
Hull	−5.05	
Bridlington	+5.40	
Tynemouth	+4.40	
Alnmouth	+4.10	
Berwick	+3.40	

Grangemouth	+4.05
Leith	+3.35
Dundee	+3.50
Arbroath	+3.10
Montrose	+3.00
Aberdeen	+2.30
Firth of Inverness	+4.45
Wick	−0.15

West Coast		
Stornoway	−4.25
Caledonian Canal	+1.00
Oban	−5.20
Rothesay	+1.10
Loch Long	+1.20
Helensburgh	+1.30
Greenock	+1.20
Ayr	+1.00
Stranraer	+1.00
Fleetwood	+0.10
Douglas I. of M.	+0.05

River Mersey	+0.05	Yarmouth I. of W.	−0.50
River Dee	−0.05	(Springs + 1.05)	
Beaumaris	−0.30	Southampton	−0.10
Bangor	−0.25	(Springs + 1.10)	
Menai Strait	−0.20	Hamble River	−0.05
Holyhead	−0.50	(Springs + 1.15)	
Aberdovey	−2.55	Cowes	+0.10
Fishguard	−4.00	Wooten	+0.10
		Ryde	+0.10
Bristol Channel		Bembridge	+0.10
		Fareham	+0.30
Pembroke	−5.05	Portsmouth	+0.15
Swansea	−5.10	Chichester (Entrance)	+0.15
Cardiff	−4.50	Littlehampton	+0.15
Chepstow	−4.20	Newhaven	+0.05
Avonmouth	−4.40	Shoreham	−0.05
Weston	−5.00	Rye harbour	−0.05
Watchet	−5.10	Dover	0.00
Barnstaple	−4.55	Ramsgate	+0.20
Bideford	−5.40		
Padstow	−5.40	*Thames Estuary*	
Bude Haven	−5.45		
Newquay	−5.50	London Bridge	+2.40
St. Ives	+6.20	Rochester	+1.35
		Gravesend	+1.40
South Coast		Southend	+1.20
		Whitstable	+1.05
Penzance	+5.40		
Scilly Is.	+5.30	*Ireland*	
Helford	+6.00		
Falmouth	+6.00	Dublin	+0.40
Looe	−6.10	Wexford	−5.00
Plymouth	−6.10	Cork	−5.50
Salcombe	−6.05	Dingle	+5.50
Dartmouth	−5.40	Shannon River	+5.40
Brixham	−5.20	Galway	−6.00
Paignton	−5.20	Donegal	−5.15
Torquay	−5.20	Coleraine	−4.00
Teignmouth	−5.20	Lough Foyle	−2.40
Exmouth	−5.15	Lough Larne	+0.10
Weymouth	−5.20	Belfast	+0.05
Poole Entrance	−2.20	Strangford Lough	+2.00
(Springs + 1.30)			

Selected Foreign Ports

Alderney	−4.10	Hook of Holland	+4.00
Bergen	−0.10	Jersey (St. Helier)	−4.55
Calais	+0.20	Le Havre	−1.20
Cherbourg	−3.20	Ostend	+1.10
Dieppe	−0.25	Stavanger	−0.50
Esbjerg	+3.45	St. Malo	−5.15
		Ushant	+5.05

Appendix 2

You wish to find out the speed at which your canoe is travelling.

1. Say you are paddling along and a lobster pot float is on the surface of the water ahead of you. From the time your bow draws level with the float, start to count the seconds (in the absence of a stop-watch try saying 'One thousand and one, one thousand and two, one thousand and three . . .' and this will give you about the right interval). Stop counting when your astern is level with the float. We will call this number of seconds T.

2. You know the length of your canoe; we will call this L feet.

3. You want to know how fast you are travelling. It is the result of a simple equation:

$$\text{Approx. speed} = \frac{2}{3} \text{ x } \frac{L}{T} \text{ miles per hour}$$

Or to put it even more simply, divide the time it takes to pass into the length of the canoe and then find $\frac{2}{3}$ of that.

4. If you want to check this:

$$\text{Speed} = \frac{L \text{ (of boat in ft.)}}{T \text{ (in seconds)}} \text{ x } \frac{3600 \text{ (sec. in an hour)}}{6060 \text{ (ft. in a sea mile)}}$$

5. Of course you will always be paddling your own 'thing' and it is always the same length (killer whales permitting). So you can go one step farther and calculate your own personal 'speed factor'.

   For instance, a slalom canoe is about 13.3 ft. long, so paddling one of these,

$$\text{Speed} = \left(\frac{15}{22} \text{ x } 13.3 \right) \text{ x } \frac{1}{T}$$

$$= 9.068 \text{ x } \frac{1}{T} \text{ or very nearly } \frac{9}{T}$$

193

N

So just divide 9 into the time it takes you to paddle past the lobster
float if you are using a slalom canoe.

6. In the absence of a convenient lobster pot, you can get a rough
   idea of your *true* speed from freely floating objects* (driftwood) if
   you know how fast the tidal stream is flowing. First calculate your
   speed relative to the chosen object as already described. Then take
   account of the water movement: add the water speed if it is going
   with you; subtract if it is against you.

7. For the best results using this system, repeat the process 3 or 4
   times so that a good *average* can be obtained.

Reed's Nautical Almanac.

Addresses

British Canoe Union, 70 Brompton Road, London SW3 1DT.
  - Write for a list of all sea canoeing clubs in Great Britain, including names and addresses of Area and Local Coaching Organisers.

Canoeing Magazine, 25 Featherbed Lane, Croydon, Surrey CR0 9AE.

Canoeing in Britain Magazine. Sent to members of the BCU, and available from Ocean Publications Ltd., 34 Buckingham Palace Road, London SW1 0RE.

Canoe Centre (Twickenham) Ltd., 18 Beauchamp Road, Twickenham, Middlesex.
  - Vega, sea paddle kits.

Capt. Frank McNulty & Sons, Victoria Road, South Shields, Tyne & Wear. Tel: South Shields (089 43) 63196.
  - Baidarka sea kayak, slalom canoes.

Gaybo Ltd., 4 Rose Hill, Brighton, East Sussex BN2 3FA. Tel: Brighton (0273) 684599.
  - Esky and Atlantic sea kayaks, slalom canoes.

Ottersports Ltd., Brunswick Place, Northampton.
  - Sea Otter sea kayak (plywood kit), canoe trolleys.

P. & H. Fibreglass Products, 70 Dale Road, Spondon, Derby DE2 7DF. Tel: Ilkeston (060 72) 3155.
  - Surfer, slalom canoes.

Saunders Educational Supplies, Commercial Street, Manchester M15 4PZ.
  - Saunseel.

Trylon Plastics, Wollaston, Northants NN9 7QJ. Tel: Wollaston (093 363) 275.
  - Sea Hawk sea kayak, canoe moulds.

Tyne Canoes Ltd., 117 St. Margaret's Road, Twickenham, Middlesex TW1 3HZ. Tel: 01-892 4033.
 – Folding canoes, slalom kayaks, canoe trolleys.
Valley Canoe Products Ltd., 4 Colwick Estate, Nottingham. Tel: Nottingham (0602) 249371.
 – Anas Acuta sea kayak, Surf Shoe, Chevron buoyancy aid, slalom canoes.
Wild Water Centre, The Mill, Glasshouses, Pateley Bridge, Harrogate, North Yorkshire HG3 5QH. Tel: Pateley Bridge (042 373) 310 or 624.
 – Surf Yak, slalom canoes.

As well as the specific items listed, all the above manufacturers sell a comprehensive range of canoe equipment.

Bibliography

ABBOTT, R., *The Science of Surfing*, John Jones Cardiff Ltd., 1972.
AMERICAN RED CROSS, *Canoeing*, 1956.
AUTOMOBILE ASSOCIATION, *Book of the Seaside*, Drive Publications, 1972.

BARRETT, John and YONGE, C. M., *Collins Pocket Guide to the Sea-Shore*, Collins, 1970.
BIRKET-SMITH, Kaj, *The Eskimos*, Methuen, 1959.
BOWEN, David, *Britain's Weather, Its Workings, Lore and Forecasting*, David and Charles, 1969.
BRITISH CANOE UNION, *Canoeing in Britain* Magazine Back copies since 1963.
BRITISH CANOE UNION, *Choosing a Canoe and Its Equipment*.
BRITISH CANOE UNION, *Coaching Handbook*.
BRITISH CANOE UNION, *The Eskimo Roll*.
BYDE, Alan, *Beginner's Guide to Canoeing*, Pelham Books, 1973.
BYDE, Alan, *Living Canoeing*, A. and C. Black, 1969.

CLARK, Mike, *Canoeing*, Canoeing Press, Magazine Back numbers since 1965.
COCK, Oliver J., *A Short History of Canoeing in Britain*, BCU, 1974.
COCK, Oliver J., *You and Your Canoe*, Ernest Benn, 1956.

DEMPSEY, Michael, *The Skies and the Seas*, Ginn, 1966.

FRANK, R., *Frozen Frontier, The Story of the Arctic*, George G. Harrap, 1964.

GUBSEN, Nicholas J., *The Nunamiut Eskimo, Hunters of the Caribou*, Yale University Press, 1965.
HARRINGTON, Richard, *Face of the Arctic*, Hodder and Stoughton, 1954.

HOUSBY, Trevor, *The Hand of God, Whaling in the Azores*, Abelard-Schuman, 1971.

HOUSTON, James, *The White Dawn*, Heinemann, 1971.

INGSTAD, Helge, *Land Under the Pole Star*, Jonathan Cape, 1966.

KEATINGE, W. R., *Survival in Cold Water*, Blackwell Scientific Publishers, 1969.

McCRACKEN, Harold, *Hunters of the Stormy Sea*, Oldbourne, 1957.

McNAUGHT, Noel, *The Canoeing Manual*, Nicholas Kaye, 1961.

MAWLEY, Robert and Seon, *Beaches, Their Life, Legends and Lore*, Chiltern, 1968.

MOWAT, Farley, *The Desperate People*, Michael Joseph, 1960.

MOWAT, Farley, *People of the Deer*, Michael Joseph, 1954.

MURRAY, W. H., *Islands of Western Scotland*, Methuen, 1973.

NATIONAL GEOGRAPHIC SOCIETY, *The National Geographic Magazine*, June 1956, Vol. CIX No. 6.

NEWING and BOWOOD, *The Weather* (A Ladybird Book), Wills and Hepworth 1962,.

PEMBERTON, John Lee, *Sea and Air Mammals* (A Ladybird Book), Wills and Hepworth, 1972.

PILSBURY, R. K., *Clouds and Weather*, Batsford, 1969.

PROCTOR, Ian, *Sailing Wind and Current*, Adlard Coles, 1964.

PRYDE, Duncan, *Nunaga: Ten Years of Eskimo Life*, MacGibbon & Kee, 1972.

REED's, *Nautical Almanac*, Thos. Reed.

ROBERTSON, Dougal, *Survive the Savage Sea*, Elek Books, 1973.

RODAHL, Koare, *Between Two Worlds*, Heinemann, 1965.

ROSS, Frank Xavier, *Frozen Frontier, The Story of the Arctic*, 1964.

ROSS, Dr. Helen, *Behaviour in Strange Environments*, 1974.

SAWYER, J. S., *The Ways of the Weather*, A. and C. Black, 1957.

SEARL, F. H. L., *The Book of Sailing*, Arthur Barker Ltd., 1968.

SHENSTONE, D. A. and BEALS, C. S. (Eds.), *Science, History and Hudson Bay*, Department of Energy, Mines & Resources, Ottawa, 1968.

SKILLING AND SUTCLIFFE, *Canoeing Complete*, Nicholas Kaye, 1966.

SPRING, Norma, *Alaska, The Complete Travel Book*, Macmillan, 1970.

STAIB, Bjørn, *Across Greenland in Nansens Track*, Allen and Unwin, 1963.

SUTHERLAND, Charles, *Modern Canoeing*, Faber and Faber, 1964.

TEGNER, Henry, *The Long Bay of Druridge*, Frank Graham, 1968.

UNITED STATES NATIONAL MUSEUM BULLETIN No. 230, *The Bark Canoes and Skin Boats of North America*, Adney and Chapelle, 1964.

WATTS, Alan, *Wind and Sailing Boats*, Adlard Coles, 1965.

WHITNEY, Peter Dwight, *White Water Sport*, The Ronald Press Co. New York, 1960.

ZIM, Herbert S., *Waves*, Worlds Work, 1968.

It.. er.. says on the chart....

KELP !

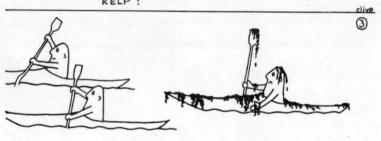

Index